Also by Noël Sweeney

Animals-in-Law

Dogs of Law

A Practical Approach to Animal Welfare Law

Bees-at-Law

Doris and the Grumpy Judge

English Hungers

An Animals' Charter

In Defence of Bees

Blue-bird sings the Blues

Jungle Judge Justice

Noël Sweeney

This edition was first published in Great Britain in 2022
by Alibi an imprint of Veritas Chambers
Unit 4 + 1 BP Bristol

Copyright © 2022 by Noël Sweeney

The moral right of the author has been asserted in accordance
with the Copyright, Designs and Patents Act 1988.

All rights reserved.

This book is sold subject to the condition that it shall not,
by way of trade or otherwise, be lent, resold, hired out or otherwise
circulated without the publisher's prior written consent in any form of
binding or cover other than that in which it is published and without a
similar condition, including this condition, being imposed on the
subsequent purchaser.

A catalogue record for this book is available from the British Library.

ISBN 978-1-872724-39-3

Dedication

For Maureen and Wendy and Polly and all the singing souls whose murmuring silence should be the siren sound that serves to make us recognise what is worth hearing. Equally they possess the rare value of sharing a creed based on a belief that is worth the knowing.

For the memory of Richard who always tried and in the attempt was never known to fail.

The Good Death	32
Stripping Stripe	34
The Bonds of Birth	37
Too Much Monkey Business	38
Baby Fae and the Baboon	40
A Pigment of their Imagination	43
Duped By Descartes	44
The Octopus Met Sisyphus	48
A Spotless Life	50
Links to the Lynx	52
A Deadhead Prize for Losers	55
Salt of the Earth	57
Cock Crows into a Cocked Hat	60
M57	63
A Gift Horse	64
A Dry Dog in a Wet Market	67
Wild Things We Think We Love You	68
Just Like Joe Exotic	72
Jumping Judge	76
Arms Are Meant To Hold You	78
Shafted By Fashion	80
Animals Circling Space	81

The Question	83
Cuckoo in the Mirror	85
Is the Polar Jury still Out	86
Toxic Soup in the Tide	88
Loose Use of Language	89
A Panther with a Panther	92
Heart to Heart	96
Prosopagnosia	98
Closing Bristol Zoo	99
No Longer Born To Run	100
Law of your Jungle	101
Jungle Judge Justice	103
A Woman and a Hat and a Black Cat	119
Written in Water	121
In Good Company	122
Pshaw he said to the Irish	124
Meet Me beneath the Magic of our Moon	126
A Fish Out Of Water	127
Grandma what is a Gorilla	128
A Green River Killer Revisited	130
The Blackboard Jungle	133
A Procrustean Apology	135

> 70% of all animal abusers have committed at least one other criminal offense and almost 40% have committed violent crimes against people.
>
> 63.3% of men who had committed crimes of aggression admitted to cruelty to animals.
>
> 48% of rapists and 30% of child molesters reported committing animal abuse during childhood or adolescence.

Men who abused animals were five times more likely to have been arrested for violence towards humans, four times more likely to have committed property crimes, and three times more likely to have records for drug and disorderly conduct offences.

The same pattern is seen in students who kill animals, often their pets. Later they might turn to murder and kill their classmates and teachers. Andrew Golden shot dogs, even his pet, before using his .22 calibre rifle to kill his classmates. Kip Kinkel tortured animals as a prelude to his shooting spree against humans. His penchant for abuse was exercised by decapitating cats and blowing up cows.

Perpetrators of domestic violence often threaten to injure or kill pets as a way of controlling others in the family. The animal becomes a tool no different than being abused as an exhibit in a science lab or fodder in a factory farm, save for them being legal. In domestic violence cases the animal is abused to harass or silence the vulnerable person who cares for her pet. For the maximum suffering the perpetrator will hurt or kill her pet in her presence. A high proportion of battered women, from over 50% to over 70%, seeking shelter in a women's refuge state their partners hurt or killed a family pet. The violent man - rest assured it is usually a man - views a vulnerable and weak person as a reflection of a vulnerable and weak animal.

The same motive applies when an elderly relative and their pet is threatened or harmed. Equally it resonates with child abuse. There may be different objects the perpetrator wishes to achieve be it financial or sexual, but the end game method is the same namely to gain control and force a victim to comply with their threats in order to avoid their pet or themselves being assaulted.

According to *The Link* animal abusers will resort to hurting or killing animals to:

Prove their power and exercise control over the family

Prevent the victim from leaving the family home or to return

Degrade the victim by forcing them to abuse their own pet

While there were no other human victims involved, it puts into perspective Kurt Zouma's assault on his pet Bengal cat by repeatedly hitting and kicking the fear-filled creature and shouting, *'I'll kill it. I swear I'll kill it.'* It is accentuated by getting his brother, Yoan, to film his violence and then arranging for the film to be on social media so it was broadcast to the world. The Zouma brothers were obviously pleased and proud of their assault on his defenceless pet cat. The Zouma brothers added a dozen laughing emoji's. When Zouma's child held her he slapped the cat in and out of the child's hands. Allied to that, neither of these characters, the Zouma brothers, seemed to have any understanding at all of the connection between racism and sexism and speciesism:

> While the victim's injuries still fester
> Indulging in a history of mass-misery
> The Zoumas betrayed their own ancestors

After the Zoumas uploaded their abuse of his pet cat, a spate of copycat crimes filled the social media. Their slavish imitators followed the Zoumas guide to being a football hero.

The view of a sharp shooter killer exemplifies the connection. A gunman went on a shooting rampage at the University of Montreal in 1980. He deliberately sought out female engineering students. He burst into a classroom shouting, 'You're women. You're going to be engineers. You're all a bunch of feminists. I hate feminists.' Then he killed a total of 14 women before turning the gun on himself. A woman who survived said, 'It was a human hunt. We were the quarry.' [*Animals and Cruelty and Law*: (1980)]

Besides even using animals in war, we also use them as disposable exhibits in space. Chimpanzees and dogs have proved to be ideal as it is easy for us to handle them and if they die on the journey that is fine. If they survive but are stricken with PTSD then they can be quietly discarded and replaced. Edward Dittmer described in *Animals in Space* how he trained and was fond of a young chimpanzee: 'I had a great relationship with Ham. He was wonderful; he performed so well and was a remarkably easy chimp to handle. I'd hold him and he was just like a little kid. He'd put his arm around me and he'd play.'

When he returned to earth they claimed he was 'grinning with happiness'. That was not a view shared by Jane Goodall, whose experience and knowledge of those animals is paramount. She said baldly, 'I have never seen such terror on a chimp's face.'

Thereafter it took 'three men to calm the "astrochimp" for the next round of pictures.' He never willingly went near a capsule again and so a different chimp, Enos, replaced him. Enos had a strap tied to his wrist to control him. Dittmer explained, 'He was smart but he didn't take to people ... They said he was a mean chimp, but he wasn't really mean. He just didn't take to cuddling.' A year later Enos died of dysentery.

Therefore, even if it was purely to protect people it is essential that we see animal abuse as serious crimes on a ladder of illegality that can and does lead to rape and murder. Pythagoras considered that killing an animal was 'murder'. Fifteen centuries later it remains true that animal abuse in childhood can certainly lead to murder. An allied feeling led Leonardo to confess: *the time will come when men such as I will look upon the murder of animals as they now look upon the murder of men.*

It would not matter if there was no such escalation and degrading graduation towards them becoming serial killers, be it more or less. Animals deserve respect because they are as Darwin found 150 years ago, 'The difference in mind between man and the higher animals, great as it is, certainly is one of degree and not of kind.'

We prefer to practise the opposite of what we preach. As a result we can willingly deprive an animal of any legal status. We are all experts in unethical martial arts. We are practitioners who hold a black belt in dodging life and truth.

Apart from the A-Z of animal law and rights and welfare, from abattoirs to zoos, from butchers to crush movies, we are left with a crucial question which is best directed at the vivisectionist because what they do is legal.

That question encapsulates all that we know about our abuse of animals and all that we need to know:

> *Question*: Why do you vivisect animals and torture them to death by your experiments on our behalf?
>
> *Answer*: The data we gain is relevant and valuable to scientists because animals are like us.
>
> *Question*: Why is it morally right for you to vivisect animals and torture them to death by your experiments on our behalf?
>
> *Answer*: The data we gain is relevant and valuable to scientists and animals are not like us.

In the *Kiko Case* [2015] an American judge, Associate Judge Eugene Fahey, decided against a chimpanzee being entitled to 'personhood' [the term for a 'legal personality' in English Law.] Later he reflected upon his decision and lamely sought to justify it.

Nevertheless Fahey was so troubled by the question of animal sentience he attempted to share his 'dilemma' with his brother judges in the *Kiko Case*:

Does an intelligent nonhuman animal who thinks and plans and appreciates life as human beings do have a right to the protection of the law against arbitrary cruelties and enforced detentions visited on him or her? This is not merely a definitional question, but a deep dilemma of ethics and policy that demands our attention.

A seven-year-old child holding her new-born kitten could have told the judge that the animal was a living breathing creature and definitely not just a thing. It was only a rankled conscience that troubled his mind and caused him to reflect and speak out at all.

Fahey's stance is pointless and pusillanimous as he looked at animals through our mirror of morality but failed to reflect on their suffering and failed to be fearless when he had the chance. Why did he not have the courage of his judicial conviction and conscience?

Fahey's stance is dodo justice in action. It is the *Dred Scott Case* [1856] revisited where American judges declared slavery was moral and legal. Save for two brave judges in that case who put their view on the line to defeat and defy the judicial pack. A similar bold stance has now been taken in an Appeal for our perpetual slaves *In The Matter of Nonhuman Rights Project v Brehen* [2022] where two American Judges, Rowan Wilson and Jenny Rivera, delivered their

A cat and a dog unto death in a crate
An 80-year-old woman on his summon
A dead body or carcass of a victim
All caught by his creed of murderous fate

Hate and love vying as a lifelong twin
So strong in him no victim could win

Albert ravished and murdered many women
Each life suspended as he determined
Each life then ended as he determined
Each one another volunteer specimen
Their future flowed through his finger's sand
As their executioner he planned his demands
Much as a shark caught on a tensioned line
Turns towards his death by a terrorist angler
Proud of his power while their lives dangled
Albert was a one-man criminal killing band
Albert sprayed each life as a tainted spangler
Tossed and twisted by their tormented tangler
Used a stiletto to slit his victim's throat
He saw a woman as his sacrificial goat
Veins pumped when their pain made him gloat
A victim's zugzwang life lassoed by a wrangler
A muscle memory kept him alive and afloat
De Salvo went hunting as The Boston Strangler

The Spin We Are In

Although we know your aim
Is to avoid our gassy methane
We are not to blame
As at heart all we do
Is the same act as you
Belch and burp as digestion starts
Then ends when we like you too
Stand and deliver thunderous tarts
Do not deceive us
When all the fuss
Is over for yourself
We are not on your shelf
All that will be left of us
Will be more stale pus

The world will still spin
Without you and me in it
The world will still spin
Each climate change minute
The world will still spin
When you forget who saves
You from sinking below waves
The world will still spin
When you are on your knees
Praying to us birds and bees
The world will still spin
When we share secrets
With the grass and trees
The world will still spin

When icebergs drown your land
A polar bear cries on faded sand
A polar bear dies on poisoned sand

The world will still spin
When sun parches your plans
Yet who among you has a clue
Whether a sea is brown or blue
The world will still spin
If we are blind in each eye
If we fail to even see the sky
The world will still spin
Out of control devoid of spirit and soul
Disappearing time's hand cannot be held
Falling fast as our failure is self-propelled
Spinning towards our desolate infinity
As the last human is stung by the last bee

PTSD

The soldier risked his life and limbs
Wading in marked waters to the brim
Joined at the hip with his every task
His honest hound followed him around
Neither hiding feelings with a mask

On their return home the fever burns
In mines and minds learned and spurned
The soldier still screams as if still at sea
Nightmare scenes that will never cease
While his silent friend shares his misery

Together they earned their lowly fee
A high price paid for a forever PTSD

A desperate mother cries in the Home
In her hour's need she stands alone
Her baby snatched for someone to adopt
Each life cut short and each soul cropped
In an instant their two hearts are stopped

A cow sees her new-born calf in a stall
In moments while she can hardly crawl
They steal her calf from her protection
The men with money use a predilection
A baby and calf split as if by vivisection

Together they earned their lowly fee
A high price paid for a forever PTSD

The mother and baby and cow and calf
Cast asunder as a tempest sea cuts two in half
Each tossed and lost and double-crossed
By us content to forget to count their cost
On our crowing compost in a permafrost

Together they earned their lowly fee
A high price paid for a forever PTSD

A door of a Home and gate of an abattoir
Revolves as each new-born is abandoned
A future destroyed and yet unquestioned
Such stolen lives which fixes each destiny
All are carved without an epitaph PTSD

Why do You Love to Hate Me

If you are neutral in situations of injustice
You have chosen the side of the oppressor:
Desmond Tutu: *The Arch*

Why do you want to make my start in life an end
Why are you packing your abattoirs with my kind
Why are you a butcher without me on your mind
Why are you a hunter intent on ripping me apart
Why are you a carnivore content to gorge my heart
Why are you a scientist aiming to vivisect my soul
Why are you a rapist ready to destroy my whole
Why are you a farmer cramping me in your stall
Why are you caging me in your human zoo at all
Why are you a pornographer selling me as a toll
Why are you a jockey whipping my frightened foal
Why are you in a sordid sex saga so my life is spent
Why are you a pornographer with a sacrificial moll
Why are you crushing me for your pervert sense
Why are you a politician killing me by your con cull
Why are you stealing lives you deem void and null

When you face Camus' judgement day
What will you say about those you flay
What will you pray as our blood spurts away
What is your vision seeing us as your prey

Burn the blindness from my eyes and let me see
Burn the blindness from your eyes to let me be
Search my soul with your justifying line of lies
Then I too will know why you love to hate me

Dog Eat Dog

Unlike the President of South Korea
Whose view is shared by one or two
Different from many of his citizens
Who treat dogs as their denizens
The President says he loves them
Only as a companion and a pet
Yet his view grates and resonates
Among those with lascivious lips
Staring at their empty plates
They say just get real
An animal cannot feel
A dog is only a dog
Moon Jae-in tries to pettifog
Instead of a pet we can get
A profit from a fast food death
Every dog has to face their fate
Being where they were born to be
In a wet market hanging straight
Then dead-eyed on a diner's plate

Farmers and restaurateurs are up in arms
Rejecting out of hand a President's palm
Trampling on their human rights
To eat whatever they want
A right to kill as a response
A few claim rights are wrong
Killing one to satisfy another
As if an animal is a sister or brother
While they hide their laughter after

Adding to the pile of burning logs
While a cage full of petrified dogs
Line up to be routinely dangled
Then and there simply strangled
All gurgling gut and minds mangled
Each stray simply skinned alive
Eyes fixed on a life now deprived

The farmers suggest a compromise
Letting the citizens eat dog meat
For only '20 years or so'
Then it can and will taper off
What a wonderful way to go
Yet given how humans behave
In 20 years dogs will be gorged
No less than they are today
The price they will still pay
Is a greasy rope in a rusty cage
A handy club and an early grave
Grasping hands reach in the trave
Each dog beaten black and blue
Will possess the same money value
Each dog lynched for their lunch
As a regular part of their daily trade
Once assessed as a bought body
Of another kind of whipped slave

Moon's intent was meant
To prove a dog was not sent
As a meal for every resident
But eating a dog or frog or hedgehog

Is the way it was and is all their days
Why otherwise were all the strays
Bound and gagged and sent their way
Otherwise they would not have been born
Much as women are meant for men's porn

All of it is where dogs were meant to be
No less natural than tuna in our sandwich
Rather than simply swimming in the sea

We Koreans see nature's gift in their birth
We alone assess what they are worth
These passing strangers on our earth
Their use for us is a verisimilitude
So morals and law cannot intrude
Ethics we can then nod and exclude
We can silently conspire and collude
Boiled or burnt or roasted or stewed
Dogs are born just to be our food
Failing to eat them would be almost rude
Your criticism of us Koreans is racist
For you English are all speciesists
Eating a cow and a lamb and a pig
Anything except one that is cute
Maybe not a horse or a guinea-pig
For us such reverse speciesism is infra dig

You have to understand we are real Korean
We are hardly going to become Pythagorean

Schrödinger's Cat

I hate water said the carp to the old trout
Who asked him what's that all about
You can't hate the thing that lets you live
Except when it is only take and not give
Wherever I move
Every river I travel through
There is never a safe place
When I am just swimming for food
All I find are barbed hooks in my face

I hate the sky said the wren to the bee
Who asked her why when you are free
Surely you can't hate your painted home
Yes but said the sickened bird
It is not what you have heard
Whenever I fly be it sunshine or rain
When I am only searching for a worm
I have to dodge bullets aimed at my brain

I hate the land said the pheasant to the farmer
Who asked him surely that cannot be true
You can't hate the space where you were born
It's easy for you but I have a reason to mourn
When I am going for a daily stroll
Rather than letting me roam free
I am attacked by gun-toting peasants
Intent to fulfil their wish to kill me

I hate the world said Schrodinger's cat to Atlas
Well how about that the seer said
As her thoughts began to swirl
As double-edged as a curved cutlass
I wonder how you can feel that way
When you have everything you need
That may seem true to you said the cat
But what you do not know
Is the hurt inside we cannot hide
My world is darker than dark
My search for shelter is spare and stark
My future starts and ends on the run
At the point of a machete and a gun
As abandoned as a church child bride
You have made my world a turning tide
No way forward and no way back
No exit or entry to your cul-de-sac
My world is a track on the road to suicide
Worst of all is your one-way ticket ecocide

Schrodinger's cat was wise to the wiles
Of ways the world can destroy our head
Perhaps the cat was right that at present
At the same time the world is alive yet dead
Does our ecocide prove beyond doubt he was
Yet we cannot prove plain truth just because
Content with our intent being sure we can hide
A present future as planned by our own hand
From committing to killing the world by ecocide
While we fail to decide if it is better to die by
The rising tide pesticide or countryside homicide

Who Breaks a Butterfly upon a Wheel

Who breaks a butterfly upon a wheel
Who among you could resist using power
To destroy some creature somewhere
For no reason except to know how it feels
Who would not find someone fragile
Then harm to induce a sly secret smile
Yes I guess we have to confess
Our power over the powerless
Captured by a never sated lust
As the archetypal man who is crushed
Where he is pushed around by his boss
Goes home to hit a woman as he is cross
Who then smacks her child for her loss
When he then kicks the sleeping pet cat
Followed by kicking a rusty crushed can
Without cause or reason other than
Using strength makes him feel like a man
Hurting someone weaker because you can
So it comes and so it goes
While second-rate Hirst art flows
A million wings broken while no one cries
Biased bars against a gaoled butterfly
Their hurt makes a coward feel real
On oh so many days
In oh so many ways
When what we condemn in other men
We practise on a sunflower stem
Spraying the harmless honey bees
Scorching the torched land and trees

Anywhere there is one more deal
Anytime there is one more life to steal
For all of us has an instant appeal
Compelled to purloin the last silent squeal
Inflicting a wound which will never heal
You need look no further than their ordeal
To see the effect of each weal
As our power is the final seal
A sound closer than the last chime peel
Hirst is not the first or the worst
Where the butterflies are broken
Without a word being spoken
Our wheels within wheels is a cloudburst
Hirst counts profits on his poverty graph
Killing a million butterflies as his epitaph
Confined in a truth that is all too real
As to who breaks a butterfly upon a wheel

Zouma and Bro Get Their Kicks

The crack of the whip
Slashes the slave's back
See how the whip crack scars
The hot horse on the racetrack

A frit father too drunk to care
About his long-suffering wife
Who he hits so hard for so long
Once again she fears for her life
Then both batter the bruised baby
Then each pet gets kicked as yet
Users and losers and animal abusers
Boot-on-boot to a pet from her accuser

Compare the Zoumas' approach to animals
Shared by the brothers as common criminals

Our silence towards the one we shun
Because the uncaged truth remains
Cain caught in a tangled human skein
Points to all of us as none of us
Care enough for fugitives forever in chains

Zouma got his kicks holding his cat
Kick after kick of his scared pet cat
As his bro' filmed their sadistic abuse
Zouma held her as tight as a noose
No reason to hide their mocking pride
Yet it is the saddest sick sour spectacle
Given their ancestors were all manacled

Treated the same as the slave ship's rat
As the Zoumas inflicted hurt on their cat
Their vaunted power over a powerless cat
Their violence towards the screeching cat
While the victim's injuries still fester
Indulging in a history of mass-misery
The Zoumas betrayed their own ancestors
Standing chained in a naked frozen coffle
An uncaged truth defeats an abusers waffle
Past sadism shared by the bro's flummery
Strapped by Massa with a leather sliver
Before being sold down the soiled river
The frightened cat's fear makes her fur
Stand on end as she shakes and shivers
Zouma made such use of so much muscle
Kick-after-kick lands with so little tussel

Compare the Zoumas' approach to animals
Shared by the brothers as common criminals

When Zouma prepared to deliver
Another arrow of hate for his bro
To film as their own history quiver
Zouma got his seven-year-old son
To hold her so he could slap her
As she struggled trying to run
Their pet cat as a speciesist victim
Yet would shout from the rooftops
About themselves as racist victims
Zouma and his bro too crass to know
After all it is only a mangy Bengal cat

Zouma's a football hero how about that
How she feels is not part of their deal

Compare the Zoumas' approach to animals
Shared by the brothers as common criminals

Zouma stands tall at over six feet three
Easier to tower over a defenceless cat
To hold her so she cannot struggle free
At 15 stone he has too much to atone
His weight is sixty times that of a cat
So easy to score and easier using force
On a cat to inflict the maximum misery

If only the cat could get her revenge kicks
Like St Paul by kicking against the pricks
An epiphany so Zouma and his smiling bro
Feels the lasting power of the law's bricks
Where the stigma of a shared guilt sticks

The First Thing we do is let's Kill all the Lawyers

The animals figured enough was enough
No longer prepared to accept such stuff
Now the gloves were well and truly off
Way past the time to start playing rough
So all at once the whippoorwill
Gave a shrill no tongue could quell
Every last one in the crowded Courtroom
Gathered all their strength together
They knew it was now or never
Their lives could only be saved
If they were prepared to sever
The complete caboodle tongues of liars
By taking a lesson from Shakespeare:
The first thing we do is let's kill all the lawyers

Then that is precisely what they did
As the roles were reversed for all time
Without a sheltered port in the storm
When the battle-cry went up as primed
Each struck with an arrowed heart
Every animal there took them apart

With strength and soul and blood pumping
Red-hot topsy-turvy and high jumping
Straight from their thumping multiple-hearts
Proving the liars and lawyers were the same
Equally they knew that they were all to blame
Each in their own way descendants of Descartes

As the Lord Chief Justice breathed his last
He asked with a plaintive plea: 'Why me?
What have I ever done except tried to be fair?'
'Ah' answered the pig with a sarcastic snort,
'This is just us with our own sense of justice
Indulging in a kind of payback-time sport
You are in our arena and we make the rules
So all humans are imprisoned in our fort
We are no longer your plaything tools
There is a feeling called belief we lost long ago
We learned the thief is a judge in a new robe
We are taking back everything you pilfered
As the self-appointed ghost of Dick the Butcher
This is your first and last visit to the future
Now is the time for us to blow you a mort
As the first criminal in our Kangaroo Court'

She fell down the Stairs

Although Jasmine and Jake
Were always on the take
They would never forsake
Their devoted pet Blake
Who was part of the family
Yet devotion did not pass
When seen by the local vet
Who raised a curious eye
As he examined her injuries
Peering at the clear screen
Shook his suspicious head
Given what he had seen
With a question that was lit
He could not ignore or forget
Evidence he could plainly see
A hidden history of Blake's injuries

He asked them as a pair
They answered together
As if with a practised story
A politician's sort of 'sorry'
Glossing over the accident
Proving how much each one cared
Her injuries were too hard to bear
On the verge of their television tears
An Oscar performance well prepared
In unison 'She fell down the stairs'

When the vet showed them the traces
Two faces went ashen as they could see
A glowing X-ray of her internal injuries

When Mabel first came to stay
She brightened up their every day
Yet in a short time things changed
They figured she seemed deranged
All she touched they had to rearrange
Her presence jangled on their nerves
Patience was less than she deserved
Patience vanished in a swift swerve
When they took Mabel to the hospital
The harassed doctor cast a critical eye
Her injuries were somewhat auspicious
The more he looked the more he was sure
The evidence was way beyond suspicious

He asked them as a pair
They answered together
As if with a practised story
A politician's sort of 'sorry'
Glossing over the accident
Proving how much each one cared
Her injuries were too hard to bear
On the verge of their television tears
An Oscar performance well prepared
In unison 'She fell down the stairs'

When the doctor showed them the traces
Two faces went ashen as they could see
A glowing X-ray of her internal injuries

They could not wait to choose
A name for their new-born son
J-J brought an end to their blues
Shared their bliss with everyone
Until his crying wore them down
J-J fell out of the cot onto the floor
Somehow crawled out of the door
Jasmine was certain J-J had crawled
Yet Jake was certain J-J simply fell
When their stories did not quite gel
The room filled with a lurking smell

The vet met the doctor who met the cops
They met a judge who pulled out the stops
With him the truth could not be fudged
Analysed the evidence much as any burglary
Choosing each pinpointed point for the jury
Who then delivered their verdicts of 'Guilty'

The misfortune of the falls
When nature and old age calls
Was brought into sharp focus
When they examined the locus
As she fell over her tortoiseshell
Together they tumbled as a pair
Granny and her pet on slippery stairs
Her worn slippers on their worn stairs

Head over heels caused them a scare
Nevertheless the doctor was quite fly
The judge was quick to probe and pry
Judging them with a certain gimlet eye

The jury heard the tale from the pair
Seeing through their story on the stairs
Judged their evidence stretched credence
Their tale of a peculiar repeat coincidence
Of an animal or child or vulnerable person
In a confined situation one always worsens
Reflected and convicted by the verdicts 'Guilty'
After the verdicts the judge delivered wise advice
He trusted would be of value in future for a life:
'Be wary and slow unless you live in a bungalow
If you see a smile signifying something sinister
Be sure to hold on for dear life to the banister
Beware of the danger of being caught unawares
By people loitering with intent at the top of stairs
Especially a pair claiming to care in their liar's lair'

A Queen's Gambit

The Russian looked at his opponent
Who stared back in slick disdain
Concealed hate under the counter
One lived without a brand of liberty
One kissed the stone of democracy
As each played their secret game
The American looked at his opponent
His eyes betraying his hatred
Each detested everything about the other
Each saw brainwashing as truth smothered
Their ideals paraded stark naked
For him democracy was sacred
The Russian and American traded
Their silent thoughts and ideals
Yet no one there
None who watched
Even knew or even cared
How the one who stares
As the centre of their game
Whose life was pawned
Without a stifled yawn
For her shining curved horn
A used stooge with no name
They neither figured the figure
Sliced limbs cracked and hacked
A life taken by a poacher's trigger
Her body blasted to smithereens
On the one-way track block
So a lie is spawned in hock

While lies are hooked and lame
Her tusk shaped as a tactile queen
The pawn in our life-long game
Those whose minds quicken
Notice the neatly carved piece
Of one whose life was fleeced
Her pain vibrates percussion
By an American and a Russian
A visible elephant in the room
A pawn followed by our spume
Her tusk as our new age tomb
A death determined in her womb
A life stolen as the poacher sang
A life ended in her shared pang
A silent clang of our zugzwang

A Living Prize

The boy threw the hoop
And caught a fish in the dish
His aim led to his claim
The stallholder handed the happy child
A plastic bag holding a trapped goldfish

The farmer edged destitution
Needed to give his life a lift
The charity collected restitution
Then bought him a tethered goat
They gave him as a lifetime gift

The answer to all her prayers
Needed to survive right now
Something to plough the field
A forced creature for a future yield
The charity gave her a burdened cow

Yet the cow and goat and goldfish
Will make them poor rather than rich
For each one will take more water
Even before they are slaughtered
When the real gift is plain to see
To irrigate the land so plants are free
Cultivate passion for work in the field
Compassion as our sword and shield

The future plan for the land
Serves to ruin time's sand

Only cultivates a mass cruelty
To deprive the fish of the sea
To confine a goat to misery
To force a cow to be a standee
The present reflects our future
Creating a problem plain to see
Careful cultivation of any society
Needs more than organically obtuse
Our mores built on an altar of abuse
Their future and yours depends on you
Reversing our role as nature's cuckoo

Life Can Get Lonely

I had no choice in my form when being born
I did not choose to lose my life to every human
Given to you when I was only a floating embryo
Dealt a bad hand seeking the dreamer's sandman
Life often gets lonely facing death and death only
Given the choice we could have been the feast
Anything except being your rising obese yeast
Or even worse a trophy-hunted weary wildebeest
I like you would have chosen to be a criminal
Selling your skin in my scheme so you are minimal
Who among you would ever choose to be an animal

Your dinner-party morals sure disappear
When you take me down to drown me
In a cascade of my fear
Hidden by your fast flood
When my heart went thud
Then spared your conscience
Ignoring my death by silence
Less a crime or even a sin
A game you alone will win
With the rattle of a charity tin
To match your long-deaf ears
A spark as a lonely heart's spear
Bursting your gushed Niagara crocodile tears

The Good Death

They have lived a good life
The trade off for being born
Followed by giving and living
Not unlike an auctioned wife
Or a slave now in her grave
After all she too is in a cage
No need to work for a wage
The bargain we have struck
Until she runs out of luck
Is to get fatter and fatter
How could obesity matter
It is a philosophical trainer
Nothing is clearer or fairer
Nothing is sounder or saner
Then again the same goes for her
When stripped naked for her fur
No different than her cuddly child
Who we rescued from the wild
Now he is finger-feeding tame
At my expense so it makes sense
When he grows fatter so easily
Now in his prime it is his time
As with his mother before him
Turning the final funeral page
Their lives shared by our sage
Plus a sprinkling of our thyme
As ever it is as a matter of fact
Almost a known unspoken pact
It is as if she knew her fate

It is as if he knows his fate
From the moment I grabbed her
Her proper place was on my plate
My money for her life was the key
Unlocked the deal to feed my family
The final test of what matters is real
Living a good life to dying a good death
Measured by how it makes us feel
No one alive could object to that deal
Even the one who provided our meal
I swear she was happy until her last squeal
I really miss her although her race was run
Yet we are keeping her memory in the family
Now I am looking forward to our next meal
Fortunately for us it happens to be her son

Stripping Stripe

Stripe was starving to death
Scattered seeds were too few
All the nuts had long gone
She flew onto the bird bath
To claim a drop of water
The builders' sine qua non
A new-build site stole her home
Nothing was left to support her
No food and nowhere to roam

She tried to lift the bin
Where the scraps were hid
The owner called her a 'psycho'
When she made him let her go
She bit him to get at the waste
A temptation of imagined taste
Was enough to keep her alive
Stale scraps to help her survive
She jumped onto the garden table
Spying food as if a treat in a fable
She bit the man holding her arm
A building site that was a former farm
Now branded as determined vermin
She balanced as a clothes line stranger
But unwelcome as a diseased danger
Caught in our trap as nature's cur
Neighbours used it to kidnap her
A prelude to their neighbour feud
To stop her hunt for discarded food

Trying to survive while barely alive
Where red is dead truth is dark and dense
An accused grey squirrel has no defence

The wandering homeless man
Held his head in his hands again
Then broke into the bungalow
To steal the bread and cheese
Without the time to ask or beg
With no one to make contact
To say 'please' or show respect
Though it was old and stale
He entered the garden at his peril
He was another kind of squirrel
Then the old homeless stranger
Ended up cold in a barred cell
Society's vision put him in prison

Paws squeezing through the gap
Bleeding paws caught by the trap
Starved dehydrated their hate sated
When her fight for food failed
She was held by steel teeth and nailed
While he only ended up in gaol
Rather than dead he was at least fed
Unlike her he was nature's red
A new home though not his own
It was a place to rest all the same
One of the two to wake up again

It is said 'Better red than dead'
Perhaps more significant that day
As an epitaph for a nomadic grey
When the barbecue smoke flew high
From one they determined was vermin
Her starvation dismissed as a false alibi
Red blood stained her grey dead eyes
As obese neighbours gorged on squirrel pie

The Bonds of Birth

The lesson of their lives
As birth and death arrives
We are descendants of Epstein
Practised in wiles of Weinstein
Caught and bartered and bought
Sold in our legal slavery
Especially by you and me
False words of welfare
Proof we do not care
For we own their world
We own the rocks we hurl
Then if it matters we rat on her
Worthless patter serves to shatter
As mean as Epstein and Weinstein
Stand in the shadows mouthing spleen
It is our earth that binds the bonds
Their birth we weigh for our worth
Killing bees to seize their honey
Killing trees to gather more money
Sell their birth to destroy their earth
Kissing goodbye to a blind eye-tooth
As valid as a practised Putin truth
Self-appointed victors stalk the earth
Possessing yet eating the purloined cake
Finished at the start by our volcano heart
Then dwell as they ache and are forsaked
We aim to break the bonds of their birth

Too Much Monkey Business

The Chinese Academy of Sciences
Now use all their advanced appliances
For a fantastic project to make monkeys fat
To make more money for a shareholder bull
Progress to move from a monkey to a fat cat
Feeding them with way too much food
So all their organs began to expand
Soon they all needed a gastric band
Obviously a band was denied to them
As the project proved making them slim
The progress of their unhealthy whim
By manufacturing a pill making them obese
Manufacturing a pill making their heart cease
Then they suffer by a massive metabolic rate
Changing from being very fat to very thin
When their bodies are blown up then shrunk
From an obese hunk to a malnourished monk
A Chinese scientist blessed by being obese
So engrossed took part in the experiment
Taking pill after pill and tablet after tablet
With a surfeit of the multi- coloured drugs
The same as he had fed to the monkeys
In no time he too became mega-obese
Taking his participation to the limit
On the path of the monkey's progress
He too lost so much weight he moved
From mere emancipation to total emaciation
Until too late he realised that an experiment
For the monkeys finished in a no-win final

When he keeled over and joined a triangle pile
To be incinerated as part of the useless data
That he intended to send to pretend to use later
Seeing the frozen startled eyes of the monkeys
As the by-products of an obese disease
Caused by him as a misguided scientist
Like him they had lost too much weight
Leaving his own lesson way too late
Before the information could be filed
Like them he was one more on the pile
From the seat of being forced to be obese
A date with an experimental fate
Locked in his own scientific end
With only zero around the bend
A cascade of carcasses on the rack
Joined by one now pinprick thin
The last of those recently deceased
Proof truth is neither white nor black
Lying with a perpetual monkey on his back

Baby Fae and the Baboon

The baboon did not have a name
Her only claim to fame
Was as part of an end game
Scientists grabbed her from the cage
Then set the instruments as a gauge
When her body was breaking
Then her heart was taken
When everyone except the baboon
Was engaged at each bloody stage
For an experiment of a high order
As they broke into a new border
A frontier with no veneer of a tear
One that had never been tried before
Then again remember it was in 1984

In time it was the saddest of sad days
When Baby Fae finally lost her fight
Even the vivisectors were in a daze
When they tried in vain to analyse
Why the experiment did not go right
Especially when all of it was in sight
As they dwelt upon her sorry plight

The baboon's body shunted out the door
As with the last one and the one before
But we should remember that was 1984

Baby Fae is remembered as one
Who was at the frontier of science

Something failed in an appliance
A baboon's heart as a misalliance
Alas no success to serenade
Even now the sadness still pervades
The minds of those on parade
Used a baboon in a masquerade
Scientists tried against the odds
To save a child survive life's rod
As it should be her name is known
By the scientists and the world
For we need to know the child
Did not die in vain
By recalling her name
Each time a scientist fights for a life
Each baby's survival on another day
Will follow a lodestar set by Baby Fae
So we can remember it was in 1984

The baboon never left the room
She was scientifically groomed
As a neo-child in a cage to perform
Her last act on an experimental stage
No one at all could recall her name
No one could remember her number
Then again why should they anyway
There was no reason before or now
When following science's holy cow
All that matters is what happens
Behind each secret locked door
The supposed prescience of science
As a talismanic manifest alliance

Slavery is freedom and peace is war
An idea borrowed straight out of Orwell
So we can dwell on our truth pell-mell
When our key opens their cell
Strikes each hour as their death-bell
Time immemorial until the next knell

For animals in 2022 at death's door
A science score of a science whore
The sound of statistics drowned
A science score for a science whore
Animal experiments as more encores
Heroes and victims of our man-of-war
In 2022 it was is and will be a turnstile 1984

A Pigment of their Imagination

On 9 March 2022
An anonymous scientist cried
When the man whose heart
He replaced suddenly died
While the pig whose heart
Was stolen for scientific pride
Has long been quietly cast aside
Another acrid statistic incinerated
Her science lab history recorded
Only a number without a name
Their interest long ago evaporated
Her present represents her past
A foreigner from another caste
A lab sample never meant to last

On May Day 2022 they checked the DNA
As to why the experiment failed that day
They found the animal they killed
The pig whose life they stilled
In order to steal her heart away
Had been stricken with a virus
From her forebears in a wet market
So the pig they used to fire us
With zeal for ending her life
Claiming a miracle by saving his life
Had been our victim who died twice
Dying first as we pleased
Dying again from our disease
Each time as we the public planned
Far from being a miracle of science
She was killed at will by a scalpel hand

Duped By Descartes

Marathon mice raced against dementia
Another slick science trick on the public
Using a horse to find fault with the cart
Scientists set on duping us by Descartes
Experiment after experiment on our exhibits
No censure by a bunch of paid benchers
Deceived by a band of research activists
Funded by a scattered scholarship upstart
We are duped by scientists duped by Descartes

All the mice were strapped and trapped
Spent their life in a free running wheel
Then raced and raced every day and night
For us to discover how they might feel
By being denied sleep or even any rest
Wires clamped on each heaving chest
While caged and then routinely enraged
Shot by a hot electric shock-upon-shock
Repeated until every last mind explodes
Electricity skeins scream in their veins
All their fixed frazzled melting brains
Fry when our virus is set to overload
To decide who were the mice slobs
Or who was the elite marathon mob
Blood running cold for a science conceit
Blood running hot for the science deceit

Yet fat or fit did not alter their fate
All were obsolete as laboratory meat

Death their prize however spliced
Destiny rolled with our loaded dice
Data gained from death could not wait
Mice paid the price of being fat and unfit
Piercing pain sliced through their wired pit
Even ultra fit mice fell by that science dice
Hard-wired inside their dazed invaded brains
Kissed by electric lips straight from the mains

An experiment meant to prove dementia
Could be aided if a patient is fit
Yet if he is pleased to be obese
Alzheimer's arrow will hit a target
In time a mind implodes bit by bit
Mice racing four to six miles day and night
Each mouse became a lab bred guinea-pig
Dying from exercise or otherwise mere fright
As each scientist ticked a box
No one cared a Faustian fig
An exhibit mouse as a rung on his rig
A grant-aided death is one more gig
Just as a dancer skips off to a new jig
She moves on to her vivisection shindig

Yet a short-sighted scientist could see
Our problem is Brutus-style writ large
Is in us not our stars given the charge
When we choose to be obese with ease
Our experiments will never cease
We can vivisect an endless supply
Of substitute mice as our sacrifice

Mice can pay the price for our vice
We can continue to eat what we please
Each mouse locked up in our laboratory jailhouse
Each mouse becomes a stuffed-to-the-gill Diogenes

Scientists meet opponents with a lance
All that matters is they get more grants
To carry out more useless research
For knowledge as a pointless perch
Selling students another classic pup
To fill an idle academic curiosity cup
Inject a hundred tame sedentary mice
Then it is true all the active ones too
Selling us their pretentious cock-up
No time for truth while bodies pile up

A phoney devotion to every false notion
Gonzo science in a perpetual motion lash-up
Mice are our constant in-house sacrifice
A tame mouse as their endless leitmotiv
In turn leaves us as mercenary thieves
Parading lies while their lives line up
Speciesist thieves as silent as a Pilate pup

Even much better if we can choose a fat rat
For no one cares about our lab abuse of that
Then in time we can progress on to a fat cat

Marathon mice raced on injected dementia
Yet scientists keep well hid under their hat
A fact that will detract as a scientific stat

Gonzo scientists stay blind to self-censure
Many have dementia and most are too fat

We find the mice to deliberately make fat
Kill them for being obese how about that
Proves the thinnest part of each experiment

Yet we do not need to kill a single mouse
Yet we do not need our scientific jailhouse
Using a horse to find the fault with the cart
Seeking an answer that needs no transfer
We know in our heart and by the mirror
We practise self-deception as our expert art
Paying scientists to resurrect his pale ghost
Dupe each other then dupe us with Descartes

One mouse or a million mice
For us it really does not matter
Death is worth their sacrifice
As long as we can all get fatter
Their sleek scientific death kiss
Borne of lies as each exhibits dies
So many killed for so much fun
A number without a reason to shun
Three million mice killed in 2021
400 years later it is still rendered
As void as a silver-bribed Judas kiss
Then as now our Gonzo expert is lawless
Still reeks of self-serving Cartesian bliss

The Octopus Met Sisyphus

Though few clung to the sharp deal
Not knowing which one was unreal
As white is black and black is white
Faded in a freezing pettifog night
Out of mind as well as out of sight
Deaf to their cries beneath the waves
Their home became a watery trave
Eight arms bobbing as a lifeless cork
Once as alive as a harpooned orca
The crooked compass for the octopus
Pointing from east unto the West by us
Her corpus plight dark yet so luminous
Fish of every kind the wide ocean binds
Closed eyes that opened our minds
To the sight we are compelled to see
Mile on watery mile of a sad cemetery
Seeing a diseased sea of animal misery

The sailors sing a shanty lullaby
While a whole world fiddles faster
Than a looming out of tune Nero
Witnessing our blooming disaster
Spies the last octopus at minus zero
When her three hearts that remain
Are broken in time all the same
All that is left from the total sum
Is our theft in an ocean of scum
As the Chinese schooners circled
Then they hacked her eight arms off

A void on the ocean's telling schroff
The mountain sunk in a seasick scrum
Hidden by the drunken sailors' rum
The throttle of so many empty bottles
Mean we can only see a plastic sea
While we stumble mumble and gurgle
All the ocean's occupants are burgled
All we can see through bloodshot sighs
All we can see is our dross demolition
When the waves drown we can protest
Then sound off for a senseless abolition
As if it was by some oceanic revolution
Rather than death a calculated destitution

Forever rolling towards our pus
Minus outweighs a plus for us
Caught by the tentacles of truth
When we ask 'where is the body'
Then try to deny our focused eye
Faint-hearted and pusillanimous
When there is no habeas corpus
Reneged on our promise to protect
Now the octopus has met Sisyphus

A Spotless Life

Mary Smith gazed out the window
Her heart was hit with a warm glow
The feeling even lit her face aglow
Seeing the first shoots rise in spring
The new-born lamb gambolling free
Such a sight made her lone soul sing
She ate at the restaurant every day
During her quiet week-long stay
Quite taken with the spotted lamb
The same one she swiftly recognised
Same time same place every day
He had a black spot between his eyes
The little lamb put on a daily display
As if pleased to be seen by her at play
Jumping and looking cutely at Mary
She smiled back without being chary
Straightaway he made her happy day
Then she was hooked in time's flow
Smith packed her bags ready to go
Still keen to see her cute little lamb
She spotted him among all the rams
At play in their gambolling programme
But then when she took a closer look
Smith instantly knew she was wrong
The black spot was in the wrong place
On the cutest lamb's still smiley face
Smith was anxious during the new day
Still worried she caught a waiter's attention
Even after a short stay in her quiet way

It was something she just had to mention
She was feeling kind of slightly bereft
She hopped nervously before she left
Whim wham she asked about the lamb
The waiter too shifted from foot to foot
The waiter seemed more than confused
Shook his head as if he had no words
Except those he knew to make her grieve
Yet now if ever was not the time to deceive
He knew those who do not lead spotless lives
Should still be able to deliver and be believed
The waiter held his steady steely gaze
Softly catching her eyes in a dull blaze
Yet the waiter was not one easily fazed
The cogs in his mind started to crunch
Not sure how to say it but he had a hunch
Delivered a kick as hard as a blacksmith's blow
Much as Judy's well-aimed rolling pin on Punch
'Why the one with the black spot between his eyes
Was the same one you munched for your lunch'

Links to the Lynx

The sleek beauty of the Eurasian lynx
We figure is rarer than a mixed mink
Though of course their coat still floats
On the back of a minx model turncoat
Yet around the year 700 we saw their pelt
Guided by our Cyclops profit-eye
We felt the umwelt would be our gelt
Mack-the-Knife style pearly teeth
We could use as a cute chess piece
Claws holding a book of our laws
Defining the lynx as a legal 'thing'
Now we are bringing the lynx back
Our environment improves by their use
Killing deer who destroy bark and leaves
Lynx strip bare with teeth that cleaves
Sharper than an inviting deer's throat
A lynx will deliver a model with a quote
To parade in a masquerade with her coat

An eco-system improves with a lynx
Besides we enjoy seeing them
Even when the countryside stinks
Then when there are too many
We can hunt them to death again
Enjoy our pinchpenny resolution
By a resort to our usual eco-solution
With empty minds when our land is full
Without looking we will find a reason

To abandon our new-found compassion
Replaced by our standard killer passion
For another commonplace 21st century cull

The beavers have been weavers
In the slow flowing River Otter
None had existed for the usual reason
Our kind of killing eco-season-treason
As they all had such shimmering fur
Plus insides of sweet tasty meat
Meant we could use them as totems
To meet and to greet and to eat
Until as usual there were none left
A bare countryside since the 16th century
Now we can let our rivers run until
We have more beavers than our fill
When once again it will be our time
To catch them in their prime
Indulge in our favourite mass-kill
No delay as carcasses decay in a land-fill

Beavers are nature's engineers
They build dams and fell trees
Reduce floods by the stream
Yet there are nature's side-effects
Their action can destroy the bees
Still that is only a small price
The real value of the beavers
Is mirrored by the value of a lynx
Compared to all an eco-rebel thinks

Yet the farmers remain concerned
The lynx will kill their lambs
Maybe the price against solid dams
The anglers rail against beavers
They kill the fish and even weevers
An outrageous act by a wild stranger
Causing an obvious devious danger
When the only ones with a right to kill fish
Are the anglers indulging in their death-wish

The links to the lynx
Is the corrosive chain
However it is rearranged
Never leads to a valid change
Hardly needs another question
That would befuddle a sphinx
When all we have to witness
We can already plainly see
Our natural face in self-disgrace
Is as nature's perpetual enemy
Check a century from now and see
How many are still living free
Or have become a mere memory
Squeezing their life with pilliwinks
A usual stance of homo sans sapience
Pound signs for pupils as our thanks
Gauged by a percentage at the banks
Their presence mirrors a natural jinx
For our life and death links to the lynx

A Deadhead Prize for Losers

Target animals denied any escape
As fish in a barrel seeing a bullet
A double-barrelled blast at a pullet
A ready-made target of holiday rape
Lurking on the hunters' landscape
Elephants are always in the room
As blatant as a mass-bigamist
Masquerading as an honest groom
In a bullet-riddled elephant tomb
As a culture creed of defined cruelty
They shoot and we by silence agree

Robin Hurt at the age of 76
Found a way to get his kicks
Boasts about how much it pays
Selling Britons an annual holiday
A safari where lives are there to take
Where all you meet are genuinely fake
Touring Africa to kill other creatures
Death is a core of the brochure features
A Londoner with a sound eye for profit
Makes sure Brits cannot miss a trophy
Big and close and defenceless to hit
How little wisdom he has learned
At the over-ripe bingo age of 76
Drips kinship blood in killing for kicks

Dickie Mac smiles and boasts about
The targets killed on his walkabout
A trophy denied to the timid cissies
Pride in his 700 trophies of 29 species

He has handily arranged to be killed
With a philosophy too readily billed
'Hunters are the best conservationists'
Which is akin to saying that scientists
Because they are degree-laden butchers
Actually conserve and preserve animals
Being butchers as well as vivisectionists
Or Putin is a model Pulitzer Prize pacifist

Abuse they dress up as 'conservation'
Language strangled beyond any meaning
Mountains of money they all crave
Pyramids of animals in a mass grave
Palmer and Vorster are bred the same
Ugly hearts without a heart to shame
Who crow about a vast bank account
Based on the head of a dead lion
Their main pride is a mane to mount
Their collective epitaph is plain
Each one hurt by nature and pain
They know they hold a trophy for losers
Of the lives they have wasted as abusers
Under a bare bulb light after a one-eyed fight
In a harsh honest 3 a.m. heat of a long night
Rest assured there is never an escape
No defence to a mass nature wild rape
A thirst for killing that remains parched
Until our politicians sate all the oligarchs
Moscow tombstones littered by bullying bruisers
We support Putin's boast 'I am an animal abuser'
Every heart-struck mirror is their refuser
Alone they fall together as their own accuser

Salt of the Earth

Humaneness is not a dead external precept,
but a living impulse from; not self-sacrifice,
but self-fulfilment:

Henry Salt: *The Creed of Kinship*

The Arch was a man and a half
Saw what was real and was not
The time he spent in England
Where he learned points he never forgot
There and then he started on his journey
Towards the blinding light of compassion
Searching through the words of Salt
He dismissed deceit as his default
Compassion was as solid as granite
Never open to compromise or lies
Never open to an easy somersault
Soon realised it was the strongest suit
The diamond had no value he preached
It was the heart that had to be reached
What he was taught he had to teach
Whether black gay gender or otherwise
Killing animals was the losers' prize
Whatever is their voice and choice
Whatever reason they have to rejoice
There is no difference in how dignity
Holds a mirror for the living and dead
As all the blood that flows from each

Is born and dies a purer shade of red
The Arch was never parched of thirst
For the bubble of rights Salt had burst
Taught him animals were not knackwurst
They could live with or without us
Their own feelings equally valid first
In or out of court more sapient than most
Salt saw the vision behind habeas corpus
The same lifeblood flowed freely in all of us

For a feeling of flying freedom
Starched in heaven as on earth
Proof of a living value and worth
Animals have their place in heaven
An epistle that is natural and too true
Whatever colour and shape of their face
Animals are not some wild deuce ace
But reserve and deserve their place
To preserve a place in their life's race
Land and sea and sky is their space
As with Salt running with The Arch Tutu
Equally while they live on the earth too

Salt had a sense of their sentience
Matched by a fevered conscience
That sailed and surpassed silence
The Arch saw the reason to exalt
Those within the clarion call of Salt
His precision of vision shared by The Arch
An unassailable truth mixed with humour
Avoiding false rumour to find a pneuma

In even a parson or a pauper or a puma
Always guarded against the cannibal consumer
Salt looked through the eyes of another
Salt saw with prescience the sadness no less
Whether it was a hurt horse or his own mother

Cock Crows into a Cocked Hat

The cock crowed since he was born
Loved by the early morning callers
Paper-boys postmen and tip-toed priests
Plus last round party-loved rock 'n' ballers
Until the day the judge would not budge
When neighbours woke a crooked grudge
Content to condemn a cock's croak to cease

A neighbour hid in the 3 a.m. rain
Ready to hear the cock crow again
The list grew longer with her name
So the crowing cock could be stopped
A blade awaited a head being dropped
He was paddling and pecking in his tracks
He saw no light of law between the cracks

No one challenged the bully-boy neighbour
Strolling around the court as cock of the walk
No one delivered any defence for the cock
Who was not given time to baulk or talk
To make any sense in his own defence
His future was forged in his past tense
When sentenced to croak his last squawk
Destined to die by bias filling the empty dock
Words he never heard struck his stopped clock

The red-faced grumpy judge listened
Neighbours who had stood in the rain
As conspirators lined up to complain

While his ears twitched and glistened
As the cock croaked his last shout out
Smug buggers smirked with satisfaction
A law of Nuisance gave them traction
Glad to have the judge share their bias
Given his typical half-baked reaction
Yet he dwelt long on what he had done
He figured and felt he had done wrong
Troubled with his thoughts in the dark
His 3.a.m. feeling with unleashed reins
What if some nosy neighbour complains
About my rescued dog's incessant bark
Still troubled if it was already too late
Will some other curmudgeonly judge
With the stroke of a pen decide his fate
What can I do now to save that cock
Or has his doodle already been docked

Neighbours presented each petty point
Huddled as a cabal to silence the cock
Echoing each other's beef-upped joint
Another dead animal to eat and annoint
All ready and able to conspire and shout
Lined up to find a cock to complain about
Branding her as a noisy countryside lout

Meanwhile the black rain lashed hard
A footloose cock strolled in the yard
A trumpet blew twice as he croaked thrice
Losing a throw of a dice with a marked card
His sound faded when a judgment was made

Followed by a funeral fugue tune softly played
While the neighbours knelt and silently prayed
While 'All Creatures Great and Small' played
The rolling wheels of law could not be stayed
Her blood dripped from the crucifixion blade
A lonesome cock strangled and swiftly slayed

M57

In 2021 a cop in Italy
Intent on arresting a felon
Was quickly cuffed by M57
So he arrested M57 for an assault
The cop put him in a barred vault
Then placed him in gaol without bail
A judge with wisdom borne of experience
Realised nameless M57 was not aggressive
Except in gaol rather than the welcome
Of his friends and the forest and freedom
Dismissing a lame lawyer's whining holler
For a few pounds bail and a forensic collar
They could track his freewheeling movements
For what was obvious to the judge
Should have been obvious to a cop
M57 should not be confined in a cell
He needed and wanted to be free
No less than chains holding you or me
Especially given he was arrested
Simply for acting in self-defence
No doubt we would all do the same
So M57 could hardly be blamed
As a matter of fact his single act
Was one both simple and true
While M57 did resist arrest
His predicament was manifest
No different if it was me or you
How you would feel clad in steel
Resisting a cop putting on handcuffs
He hit the cop once to make him stop
M57 acted as any grizzly bear would do

A Gift Horse

See the bright blood in the snow
Mixes so well with the flow
Now the fire's caught fast by the flood
There's much too much snow in her blood

Red clouds of dust fill the phial
Her face saves no trace of a smile
Her purple lips suck one more breath
Her vein's kissed by our Iscariot of death

Pull the lever that sends the shock
Make it max while they are in hock
We have to conceal our addiction
An electric cure for our infliction
Line up all the caged exhibits
So we can be as ever chrematistic
As well as academic and voyeuristic
Yet equally become more egotistic
Collect the data from our statistics
A prize for our science community
Our glee revealed by their ecstasy
One million repeated experiments
To add to the millions already spent
As head and heart is twisted and bent
Each head and heart is a broken token
Mixed-up in a torrent of our torment

The torture is rough and gets rougher
Anything as long as we do not suffer

Smoke plumes drift and hit the sky
The carcass of one who had to die
A blade cuts a line on the mirror
Each sliced for our junkie whim
A bargain as each scientist finds
Another exhibit as one more victim
True value as an animal pays the price
A bargain as we win and they lose their skin
We get the presents as they pay the penance
For us an absence counts for so much less
Than our scalpel demand for their presence
The expert leads the exhibit to their death
Each expert borrows morals from Macbeth

Let's inject the poison in our veins
Let's addle our brains with cocaine
Then we can vivisect caged animals
Then we can free all our criminals
Claim it is an illness not a crime
A useless lie to protect our paradigm
Our pain in them is no contradiction
For our predilection of our addiction
As we inject more and more snow
A needle and a rush of the red flow
Send millions of innocent creatures
As our favourite science features
Their blood being spilt for our guilt
An excuse in our false solace of skunk
Dead-head conscience as our legal junk
Then no one who counts can ever flunk

Using a premeditated animals mega-death
Our daily doped doppelganger ersatz death

See the bright blood in the snow
Mixes so well with the flow
Now the fire's caught fast by the flood
There's much too much snow in her blood

A Dry Dog in a Wet Market

Scavenging on the street for something to eat
Anything whether it was sour or sweet
Hoping to escape from the people's wrongs
When caught by a gloved human tong
Then strung up in a crowded cage
Saw her as part of their weekly wage
One by one turned each life's stage
Dog after dog taken without a care
Until she was the last one huddled there
When they tried to grab her she resisted
The more they used force with a cruel twist
Catching her hard with the jagged tongs
So her pangs were sharp and prolonged
A matter they held without a heavy heart
For the more the pain the more the gain
The higher the heat the sweeter the meat
So the stray struggled as they juggled
With her will as the prize in their eyes
Which she wanted to do all she could
To stay inside the stained cramped cage
As her last ditch wish to deprive
Them of their wish to thrive
On one more dry dog to disbud
Drenched in her own spurting blood
In the wet scarlet market place
Served to dribble down their face
For if they ever got her outside
She would become someone's insides
She knew as sure as eggs is eggs
She would have no chance to survive
Against their intent to skin her alive

Wild Things We Think We Love You

In 2022 a herd of bison
Were being released
In the woods of Kent
To reintroduce the bison
Where their ancestors
Were exterminated by us
Only 6000 or so years ago
But now
We can forego their woe
Vaccinated with renewed passion
With no reason for us to be riled
For any of the species in the wild

Although it is not quite that simple
As bison kill the bark and eat trees
As the lynx before them with bees
Rub their thick fur against the trunk
Shifting where the bees lurk alive
A deadwood home for the woodpecker
While we can still fulfil our role
As a self-appointed countryside wrecker

The wild cats are alive again
Basking in sun drenched Scotland
Which is slightly odd as it is said
Domestic and wild cats are inter-bred
A peculiar species of a different kind
If the experiment is a success
Then they can live again in Devon

Safe from gun-toting poachers
On a short step to a rural heaven

Then again even if it fails
Our sterling ship still sails
We already have the past proof
Wild cats went through the roof
With a feeling of perverse pride
As before England will decide
To follow a prejudiced distinction
Then hunt them again to extinction

Long ago in the 18th century
The last white-tailed eagle
Flew through English skies
Disappeared as the last one died
At our hands throughout the land
Persecuted by us as perpetrators
We figured they harmed other birds
That was the root of their destruction
As we wanted to be the only ones
To kill the smaller birds for pleasure
After all what were bullets made for
Except our partial penchant for leisure
Except for our use in war and killing
Caught by us as the wild and willing
People and birds as sheer fun
For you and me and everyone
Except of course the dead eagle
Yet who cares when killing is legal

Now we intend to reintroduce
The supreme white-tailed eagle
In Scotland and the Isle of Wight
We have somehow seen the light
Much wiser to split the magpie miser
Then in time as is our constant way
When the new visitor has outstayed
Their welcome in crowded skies
They end up in crisp fresh pies
Use our bullets for a new war
What else are bullets made for
Except killing us plus other animals
As a rabbit is their rarebit
Each a ready-made target
Patiently awaiting a casket
Longing for a drooling retriever
To return with a heavy mouth
Then fill another empty basket

In the UK we have had no bears
For well in excess of 1000 years
Hence we had to be content
With a second-rate sense of bull-baiting
People denied their natural inclination
To draft stories about bears in the wood
Chain and train them to dance for us
As Elvis was a human dancing chicken
For Colonel Tom and his finger licking
Hot plate device that made them holler
Elvis and the chickens learned to dance
As the Colonel counted mounting dollars

Forget the squalor and dance in the parlour
Then when the dance is over
We can unlock their chains
As our new slave beyond their time
The song and dance rots at the stem
Surpassed by our need to kill them
Then the only ones who really care
Cannot say as they are all dead bears

Just Like Joe Exotic

The Tiger King has a sordid ring
Joe Exotic pumped and preened
Across our distorted screen
Running a zoo for a bloated fee
Paid for by people like you and me
Yet when we see tense-eyed tigers
Cramped and crowded in cages
Manic strutting as sad stereotypes
Mange-ridden on shrunk stripes
Conservation by a phoney hype
Stress level rising through their rages
Tigers as tight as tinned sardines
Seeing the same scene-after-scene
We can feign and start to be startled
As if until then we did not even know
A glaring truth of all we gleaned

The trophy farmer's face contorted
When he steals new-born tiger cubs
Away from their perplexed mothers
Within days of their giving birth
Our betrayal as their purpose on earth
He ignores the low muffled cries
Of the cubs and of their mothers
As PTSD bites with no goodbyes
Two shattered hearts wither and die
As with those before and to be next
An endless chain links a vexed text
Serving to fill every vacant place

A hunter shoots into any scarred face
Under cold suns with smoking guns
A failed grace as our own silent sext
Blasted away by our double pretext
Between the darkness and the dusk
Hear and see the hollow howling husk
Of our tainted values writ large
Of surrendered lives without charge
Of 70 billion animals hour-on-hour
All fallen by our unleashed power
Slaughtered for their bodies and ours
Most bound together in factory farms
Where we harm them without alarm
Out of our sight we keep our meat
Far away from a natural vision-seat
Tiger cubs crying as stolen calves
Wrenched from a grieving mother
A matter of hours after being born
The cries of the mothers drowned
Their calves are swiftly taken down
We condemn the trophy hunters
As we chomp a juicy T-bone steak
Together with all the other punters
A life we decide is ours to make or break
A life we decide is ours to stake or take
Shoot wary birds escaping towards the stars
Then condemn those leaving dogs in hot cars
While farm animals are lifted then shifted
Across countries being hit by heat
Then onward to an arctic freeze
Our ice-cold hearts match bodies we seize

Our closed souls match closed cell gates
As corpses end on our cleaned dirty plates

Hear tantivy profits grow click-clack
Another racehorse killed on the track
A whip-crack spine and a broken back

Choosing to look the other way
Never linger over or even stay
Their dead bodies are true semiotics
Animal signs are our choice narcotics
Although we can try to deny
Signs that are an eternal proof
We know we are far from fireproof
For it is no manufactured spoof
We know with our hero Spartacus
Ideals flung under a passing omnibus
No voice to raise a rumpus or fuss
Alive or dead they are not one of us
Goodbye to the wisdom of Aurelius

No way to shore up the dam
Until the last animal alive
Is our final sacrificial lamb
An A to Z of the species we tethered
Each one serves us as a bellwether
Aware we are all in it together
When the abuse courses in our veins
Running through to remain osmotic
At once assume being routine despotic
A pale imitation of our hero Spartacus

A paler imitation of a marked Aurelius
Passing it off as naturally neo-neurotic
Each of us are voluntarily concussed
Masked emotion disguised and robotic
Who as true parasites are never symbiotic
In our unquestioned pain-drenched hearts
We know we are all just a perfect demotic
On a pixie-path to become Joe Exotic

Jumping Judge

The prosecution jumped up to claim
The animal was rived with pure guilt
Every point used to persuade proved
Her culpability was beyond the hilt
Every word they heard made them wilt
For they knew how the court was built
By bricks of bias and mortar of prejudice

Animals were asked about their defence
All they could do was shrug in silence
Jumped down quicker than they jumped up
Because they knew as with their kind
Justice never had any of them in mind
For them it was deaf gagged and blind
Always supping from a Socratic cup
No surprise they were sold a human pup

Then the jumped-up judge jumped up
As usual he was in his overflowing cups
His ruddy face blotched by too much port
Killing for fun was his favourite sport
Killing was his practice in and out of court
When he looked at the assembly of animals
He screamed 'We know all about your sort.'

Scratched the huge wart on his bulbous nose
As he sentenced the whole lot to be aborted
He went to jump down to jump up then curled
The animals realised at once that he repeated

Everywhere to everyone within our world
For in the past and present and the future
His world made their world a judicial suture

Arms Are Meant To Hold You

The diner considered he was a culinary expert
Bored and tired of eating average food
He wanted something to excite his jaded palate
He opened a restaurant with a great deal of fuss
With a tank full of fish of every description
Though the main exotic offer was an octopus
He was so inventive he called it 'Octopie'
He intended to pluck the creature from the tank
Hack off her arms to watch her slowly die
Then place her on his plate
As that was to be her fate
Swiftly become part of the diner's face
He looked as happy as a sandman
At least that was his plain plan
When they sat down and quietly waited
When he plucked the octopus out
They licked their lips waiting to be plated
Then truth to tell he slipped
Then stumbled and fell pell-mell
The octopus reached and grabbed his neck
Suddenly in seconds he was held by an arm
Then two and all eight of them
Each springing from their body stem
Eight arms in a stranglehold so tight
He could barely begin to put up a fight
The more he struggled the tighter the grip
There was no slip betwixt the cup and lip
As the octopus caught his bulging eyes
A choice in the moment could be realised

Presented to him by the diner's cute fall
To win the fight in a final choice all in all
The expert spread out across the floor
Sheepish diners slipped out the door
Seeing the predator had eight arms
Was enough to resist her charms
Although he had wanted no fuss
That was what he got because
It was a one-sided ruckus
Though a lot of them cussed
Most never bothered to visit the restaurant again
The most they did was attend his funeral in the rain
Indeed no one there tried to eat any octopus again

Shafted By Fashion

Standing in your furs 'n' your feathers 'n' minks
Your Old Lady takes one too many drinks
Your Daddy is a lawyer who defends kinks
Your brother hangs around with all the finks
Oh boy! I'm shafted by your fashion
I'm laughing so much there's onions in my eyes
You're living proof love is just a spoof
And I wish you were shafted too

Standing in your leather and rainbow suede
All that you are wearing from lives betrayed
Tricked and trapped as part of your trade
Stained by a price that will never be repaid
Oh boy! I'm shafted by your fashion
I'm laughing so much there's onions in my eyes
You're living proof love is just a spoof
And I wish you were shafted too

A life based on a want you never need
A life patterned by a passion for speed
A life cursed being born with a bad seed
Try finding a fashion that fails to bleed

From finishing school to the servant's bell
An accent that chimes with a hangman's knell
A hand-me-down remnant to a ne'er-do-well
Visit the banshee when your head starts to swell
Oh boy! I'm shafted by your fashion
I'm laughing so much there's onions in my eyes
You're living proof love is just a spoof
And I wish you were shafted too

Animals Circling Space

A dog smiles with handcuffed teeth
Fixed with a grinding induced fear
Facing death without a wreath
Her gaping mouth forced open
Struck in shock with a silent scream

The rocket hurtles in a slipstream
A black heart hole of hollow space
Her confusion on our fusion scheme
Is etched deep on her panicked face
Her nightmare living our idle dream

Round and round for a million miles
A dog replaced by a manacled monkey
Still fixed with his death-mask smile
A volunteer exhibit is found and bound
Twisted through our master race turnstile

The scientists claim their honours
Then bask in the glory and fame
Though the dog and monkey fades
No experimenter knew their name
For that would mean an identity
As they sail in our sad space sea
Sailing forever in a cloudy future
A black hole serves as a ligature
Circling for us as a stoned Sisyphus
Caught between science and society

Expendable objects in our space race
A shooting star of man-made misery

A small step for mankind
A false step as a blindside
A one-way trip to Mars
A trip to the marred stars
A lottery ticket for a life
A life of pure trumpery
A loss we win by usury
Laika a stray mongrel stolen on a Moscow street
Forced to circle the earth under a callous moon
She died terrified inside a Russian rocket at Noon
Laika a sacrifice in six hours for a science perjury
Animals handcuffed to our shallow space sorcery

The Question

I feel that animals are as bewildered as we
except that they have no words for it.
I would say that all life is asking:
"What am I doing here?"

Isaac Bashevis Singer

As with a terminal cancer
When there is no answer
Yet death has its own story
For we seek a sort of glory
Killing other creatures as a whim
A cull and profit our pseudonym
Even if gain is our holy wine hymn
Our autosuggestion denying rights
Demand for ourselves alone
Cuts others beyond the bone
Yet is wrong and can never be right
Asking, 'What am I doing here?'
Rest assured they are sure
They were not born to be forlorn
Or to be a perennial human thorn

Why do you figure you are blessed using a word
It could be nature's curse you have not heard
Stealing their song is not what kills the songbird

Our trump cards on the table
The supposed soul we borrow
From a self-ordained religion
Is only a ploy by us to avoid
Asking the ultimate question
We share with a polar bear
Plus every raggedy pigeon
A corpse of truth laid bare
Sitting on our judgement chair
A natural bias naturally unfair
An arrow of lies we can never retract
An epitaph proving our ego is intact
On our shadowed idea we sell as a fact
Living a lie trips easily off each tongue
Hidden as an ambitious politician's bung
Using our falsehood deeds undercover
To conceal so others do not discover
Though we know it is pure sophistry
Burning trials and witches against her
A passé-partout we pretend is true
We alone are a nation of animal lovers

Cuckoo in the Mirror

They come along as burglars
Then for no good reason
Without cause or provocation
Whatever the time or season
Rob the guileless bird of her song

Every day in trees and woods
Using force and strength at best
They steal all they want
Then dump each bird from their nest
Camouflaged by woods and trees

Killing is their trade
Trade is now so good
Suspended on the coop
Ever ready to swoop
Under a winged hood
Killing birds who cannot move
Fledgling birds are never safe
The burglars serve to prove
Action before she flies the coop
Calling and committing a coup
As a bird drops before she even grew
Nature's mirror detects the one who slew
Behind the guise of the quisling cuckoo
A serial killer lurks whose feelings flew
Nature's mirror reflects a reason for rue
The culprit's identity is drawn on a flue
A blurred image we recognise of me and you

Is the Polar Jury still Out

The snow white real teddy bear
Looked at the melting ice-cap
Then wondered to herself
Whether anyone anywhere even cares
She figured everywhere I look and see
As the blinding sun almost blinds me
Is our life vanishing along with my liberty

Now I have nowhere to live
I have nothing left to give
All I had last year has disappeared
I have no more companion bears
Heat destroyed the freezing air
Everywhere I look now is bare
I have neither food nor seaware

As victims of a human warfare
My present is now threadbare
My future dying as I am relying
On nature's invisible welfare
A chain recycling and supplying
One I still fail to understand
Why you are stealing my land

You confine me as your albatross
Yet you gain so little by my loss
A bent two-headed coin you toss
To render me to your underworld
To spout a shibboleth on my death
Words as hollow as my last breath
What is your gain as I lose my world

Now there is no snow white ice
But only a blinding solar sun
Shining through my translucent soul
A helter-skelter rollercoaster stun gun
I wonder if I am the last polar bear
Crushed by your runaway steamroller
As you stand and stare devoid of care

For all your hard acid rain talk
Where bears cannot win or walk
It is way beyond the time to ask
'Whether the jury is still out?'
For none of you are up to your task
The question shows you do not know
What it is about when you are the tout

The question will freeze upon your lips
The question is answered drip-by-drip
Instead of asking about a wildlife plight
Who wielded the knife causing us strife
Maybe we could ask the jury about
Why there is now no longer any doubt
Against you we will lose any contested bout

Asking any question about your jury
Forgives yourself and forgets our fury
It is a pointless potpourri of original sin
Our future is more than dire
Our whole world is on fire
You hide in the porch with a blowtorch
So your forever jury cannot now be out
Impossible to answer as they were never in

Toxic Soup in the Tide

The spilled sewage flowed free
From factory to river to the sea
Hour-after-hour week-by-week all year long
No one caring whether it was right or wrong
The mass polluters were well known
Here and there and everywhere
They were or happen to roam

The sewage flows in a soupy loop
Chemicals of all forms in the group
Water turns colour with no solution
Fish farmed disease an unnatural evolution
From factory to fish to cancer as our coup
A story to ignore as no one wants our scoop
As we await a self-created virus revolution

We can sup with the dictator devil
Using a long Putin table and rusty spoon
Knowing it will never be on the level
There is no guide for a freedom ride
If we decide to sup with a tainted spoon
Our toxic soup washes up in every tide
Until the time beckons us all too soon

Eyes still fail to see past evil swill
That serves to shine but exists to kill
Hiding the beauty of an invisible moon
Although we already know a toxic truth
There is no one among us ever immune
As we willingly sip the poisoned soup
With our own spiked Putin spoon

Loose Use of Language

When the wise judge said
'Your words are a disguise'
He saw through our lies
We call it a 'trail hunt'
But our words are bent
To put you off our scent
To fool smart sabs
Get our grasping dabs
On the throat of Charlie
Before our hounds at the scene
Blocked rocks as our smokescreen
When we see a fox rest assured
We give the world our word
An 'accident' somehow happened
A coincidence he never escapes
The hole happened to be blocked
We see fear in her eyes is locked
The art of killing is our weathercock

The tune in our mind jukebox
Is to despatch every last fox
We know the 'trail' is a lie
As honest as blowing a whale
Harpooned from the ocean sky-high
Our hounds at his throat in the fight
A sweet delight sets our hearts alight
Our appetite will be fed
When every fox is dead
Nothing rocks like a dead fox
Believe me you except for two

We train hounds to break her neck and will
Their teeth ensures our game ends one to nil

As they rip her apart
We storm down the hill
Ripping her to shreds
Is better than any pill
However many we kill
We will have a void to fill
We will never quit until
Every last fox is stilled
We will scour the scorched earth
To find some other thing to kill
Then feign it is 'class warfare'
Because in love and war
Every action is deemed fair
To satisfy a hole in our soul
That remains empty until each day
We can grab her and have our way
Her last long helpless scream
Her hot nightmare is our dream
We need some sort of strife
Excite a light in our humdrum life
Hunting is our daily prayer
Why we keep repeating our fanfare
Our critics indulge in 'class warfare'
As it is a line
We will not hide
We will be a pesticide
Dripping for their stillicide
Killing everything in our path
The wisdom of our wrath

Fox or hare or stag or anything at all
Steal their heart while they all fall
To satisfy destruction of wildlife
We can then live our lustful life
Our birthright gene is their genocide
We are self-serving natural-born killers
We will bring our own culls on
Until the last wild animal is gone
We will force their suicide in our stride
As warriors of a red-claw countryside

At the Ball we all make small talk
Laugh as a gurgling drain in the mud
Our excitement seeing their life-blood
We count how many lives were lost
We count how we won without cost
Drowned by our laughter as thereafter
We will boast how the fox was toast
When we loudly toast her death
With the unborn cub inside her
Sacrificed by fright right beside her
A glass of wine and a magnetic shrill
The fox as lonely as a whippoorwill
A toast as a boast for the next fox ghost
As we plan the thrill from our next kill

The trail hunt is the reason we thrive
Existing so a fox will never survive

A Panther with a Panther

In 2022 in downtown Brunswick city
Their acts resonate without pity
Ahmaud Arbery was hunted
Three men beneath cold stars
Tracked him in revving cars
Strapped in by their trap
Travis McMichael held him
Too close with his loaded shotgun
Outnumbered with nowhere to run
Shot three times at close range
His chest blown away by the blast
In seconds Ahmaud breathed his last

Ahmaud was part of their jape
So one thing was for certain
Their trophy behind the curtain
With no need for a crystal ball
To see he would never escape
Downed by McMichael's bullets
Finger poised on the trigger
An itching honky pulled it
One two three burst bullets
Ahmaud fell as a poacher's victim
Ahmaud's life skimmed on their rim
Caught by their bias and vigour and vim
In the night justice grew dim outside him

Month after month passed without arrest
While the three hunters escaped justice

Ahmaud was not one the cops missed
Doing nothing was their practised bliss

Self-defence became McMichael's claim
Indeed a justice card was the trio's game
They had no intent to hurt him or maim
He was a stranger they saw on the street
Figured he was some unwelcome dead-beat
They followed tracking his pounding feet
Paced him moving to their own drumbeat
He had no chance to flee let alone retreat
In an instant he had no heartbeat
Blood flowed from his head and feet
A problem was their lies were liquid
The video showed what they had hid
Dylan wisely noted with no guile
'Look out kid, it's somethin' you did'
With a D.A on his track and their style
Meant the killing had to end in a trial

McMichael squirmed as the questions
Demanded answers on his sworn oath
Half answered with truth's indigestion
All he was asked was too tough a task
Then again when being cross-examined
Hung on hooks by an advocate sleuth
McMichael found no escape route
Ahmaud in reverse in their pursuit
They could not find lies to refute
Caught by the questing law's claws
A single unassailable nailed truth

The judge was fixed in his sentence
'Life' for the one they had taken
The same one for each of the three
Now serving time in the penitentiary
While young Arbery spends his time
In a mahogany overcoat for their crime
Six feet below in a cold earth cemetery
It was Bobby Seale's oft cited claim
Black men were white men's fair game
From Ahmaud Arbery to George Floyd
Remains the same of a life destroyed
A line that stilled the life of Emmett Till
Is a soiled memory that lingers forever
Finger-pointing at killers as lawgivers
In the flowing Medger Evers river
Their rednecks and their clan
See black people as criminals
To be accused and abused
Then held in a roped noose
Much as we see all animals
To be abused and used
Being amused for our use
Never let loose without an excuse
Their clan strung up the dog too
Proof what they knew to be true
A philosophy borne of warped pride
A black man and his dog side-by-side
Each noose a different kind of caboose
On the wrong end of the crowded train
Yet the feeling induced was the same
Animal or black on a one-way track

The deal between the panthers
Is a question hunters never ask
They move with a defined rancour
For the panther and black panther
To them is just the same
Prejudice is their anchor
A politician's swivel-eyed shame
Rely on us to play a crooked game

Heart to Heart

We are supposed to marvel at a miracle
Of a genetically modified pig manacled
Who becomes a blind scientific spectacle
As her body is poked pricked and probed
As her organs are prodded and daubed
Then her life becomes their obstacle
Finding a human heart as a receptacle
So the man who was saved
At least had a voice and a choice
So his decision was fair and free
Whilst the pig was only an exhibit
Whose life had no intrinsic value
Except for her use to you and me
For science to reach the pinnacle
Is all that matters for their miracle
Do they wonder what they would do
If no animals for experiments existed
Or it was illegal for scientists to persist
Would their routine minds stay vacant
With their vulture culture as complacent
Or be forced upon the pursuit of truth
Following a path of fairness and justice
Where we spared her life from just us
When they were forced to find means
By scouring all their alphabet genes
Equality would be unequivocal
Honest and fair and reciprocal
From our path towards injustice
Would not be defined by science

Pointless in part and useless as a whole
Selling a religious lie only we have a soul
Buying into an animal's use to us
But by a principle that is spiritual
Dignity is a code of a moral ritual
Borne of respect rather than habitual
So even Cartesian hearts were tactual
Now that would be a certain miracle

Prosopagnosia

The inability to recognise faces is a splendid gift
From some idol deity to give our lives an uplift
We can abuse animals from birth to death
Before they are born until their last breath
Cuddling the cute ones and eating the rest
Their arms and legs and right to their breast
Over and beyond those points in our favour
We can enjoy their company and yet savour
Each sweet and sour taste and their flavour
Morality is something we can simply sift
For god or some prophet has provided a gift
Ethics has no purpose and causes us no rift
We spend their lives using our daily thrift
So prosopagnosia is our best anaesthesia
An instant solution for abuse by amnesia
The swift gift we can use without a trace
No guilt or remorse of any sort in its place
As we forget the feelings with no disgrace
Forget who we killed in our consumer race
Yet without a mirror being near or anywhere
The corpse wears a look that reflects their fear
Created an ocean of hurt without a single tear
Our conspiracy that animals are our volunteers
Near their end we can play at being cavalier
Though we know we are impostor musketeers
For the first time we see in them a true base
A gift of an image of our human face
Seeing the problem we solved as our wirra
We avoided our lies by smashing the mirror

Closing Bristol Zoo

How the people cheered when they heard
Zimmerman's announcement that
'Bristol Zoo is closing down'
He had hardly uttered those very words
Before the grapevine celebrated the end
Of a hated place as an Animals' Alcatraz
No escape from the whooped razzamataz
Yet inmates had not committed a crime
Forced being born to live and serve their time
The joy exploded when his words were loaded
Zimmerman said it was a 'conservation charity'
It was only closing where it was located
It would soon be celebrated as a charity
Proving that as usual the goal will grind
When you see the goal that lurks behind
A facade that imprisons those
In caged cells that are closed
Without even looking prisoners will find
Zoos caught in a time-warp of closed minds
Zoos are run for us with a time that binds
With no key and no freedom from me and you
A pervasive panic on the face of the walleroo
Our disgrace drawn on a face of the wanderoo
Until a last breath guarantees a release by death
Proving what we knew all along to be true
In or out of a cage our world is a human zoo

Yet in Bristol Zoo animals are conserved
Now many Horfield Prisoners have reserved
Their next sentence there as they deserve
A sight for scarred eyes through barred stars

No Longer Born To Run

She is too old to be of much use now
A champion to one without a pantheon
Age has frittered her fitness somehow
She once was a fine athlete
Now she awaits her lonely fate
No visitors no cups no cards
From a Home to a lonely graveyard

Her legs are weak
Her gait is unsteady
Her speed has long since gone
She is getting frailer by the day
Even her sight has faded away
No one cares about her now
As pointless as a milk-less cow

Lifelines etched on her face
Nothing is rewarded now
All the money has faded
All the memories are erased

You do not need to be a bloodhound
To see the bounce between any senior
As each is unwanted and stands alone
Abandoned and as real as a dead clone
Seeking a chop and home of their own
A pale perfection of our confection
Her day in the sun and her race is run
Mirrored on a moneyed merry-go-round
Stopped short in her tracks by a stun gun
A vernier value of any unwanted greyhound

Law of your Jungle

Anyone with a hoof
Instead of a hand
Or no hand but a paw
Lives below your law

Whatever is your politicians bungle
In the serpentine law of our jungle
Skin in the game as a legal mongrel
We can brag with a meaningless saw
No one under the sun is above the law
We are willing to make an exception
When we consider the mass reception
For those whose voice is a hee-haw
Or whose grip is a fur mitt or a maw
Forever lost in our alienated land
Unable to grasp our withheld hand

Given your testament is fudge
Let me give you a slight nudge
As to whom I choose to dodge
When your hate lodges as a wodge
In the mind of your own kind
All we meet and always find
People who dress to impress as a judge
Your law is a veritable man-of-straw
For your vision is my blood in the raw
Selling us as tarnished dross by your law
A shiny slick sight is your glittering flaw
We both know would not fool a blind jackdaw

Jungle Judge Justice

Jungle Judge Justice

Philomena Phucketyall [PP] was a ruddy-faced corpulent lawyer who became a middle-aged judge. Day after day she dealt with run-of-the-mill deadly dull cases involving shoplifting and speeding and the odd domestic dispute. The work load bored her to tears. She held on as she was soon due to get a fat pension that would allow her to live the life of Riley and luxury while idling her time away boasting about all her triumphs in the cases she had been involved in and her numerous animal trophies over the years.

Samantha Shytehawk [SS] was a ruddy-faced corpulent lawyer who became a middle-aged judge. Day after day she dealt with run-of-the-mill deadly dull cases involving shoplifting and speeding and the odd domestic dispute. The work load bored her to tears. She held on as she was soon due to get a fat pension that would allow her to live the life of Riley and luxury while idling her time away boasting about all her triumphs in the cases she had been involved in and her numerous animal trophies over the years.

PP and SS were firm friends and had been for almost forty years, at least on the surface.

From January every year PP planned her long holiday which was to get out of her 'comfort zone' with her Royal friends and acolytes and fellow parasites where she would blast birds from the sky, kill every manner of fish and execute every wild animal that passed her path. She always went with SS.

SS was a mirror-image of PP in fatness, lack of fitness and especially finding salvation in killing any animal that was caught in their cross-hairs. If any animal was on the land or in a river or flying high in the sky, PP and SS would be openly glad to kill them for the pure pleasure and open satisfaction of seeing the animal die. They seemed to feel it was almost their duty to do so.

As killing beavers and bees and birds and squirrels and every kind of feral creature they crossed was the first interlude to their introduction at home, their real thrill was going abroad and killing endangered animals. Although they knew that the law had been changed so being trophy hunters was illegal, that did not bother or fuss them at all. After all they were the primary lawyers. They had such a vast network of connections including other legal eagles and politicians in their pocket.

As a result they went on their usual animal trip to Africa intending to slaughter every animal that crossed their path. The bigger the better and the strongest was the best one of all to catch off-guard and trap and instantly kill. They envied the obese American dentist, Bronkhorst, who voraciously slaughtered Cecil the prized African lion for no better reason than he could and had more money than morals.

It was not too difficult as PP and SS had a guide and a powerful weapon that could demolish a house as if it had been hit by a hand grenade. So there was no danger to themselves, the endangered species were driven to an open pasture where they ate meat laced with drugs which rendered them drowsy. All the animals were then caught in their collective cross-fire. Any animal's pain counted for nothing against their pleasure. If on an odd occasion any pain was weighed their pleasure always tipped the scale.

Then PP took aim and blasted the huge beautiful harmless elephant into eternity.

Then SS took aim and shot the jungle king shaggy-haired lion so full of holes her blood squirted out in a waterfall that caused her to drown towards her death.

The swift demise of the elephant and the lion before their eyes was 100% satisfaction guaranteed just like the holiday brochure claimed. It was exactly what they had paid for, an experience and memory that would last a lifetime.

Back in England the Daily Criminal List was finalised and posted at Crook's Corner Crown Court. The first case was against PP who was charged with killing an elephant.

PP appeared before Judge SS. She pleaded 'Guilty'.

Basil O'Doore [BO], the lawyer representing PP made the usual insincere submissions in mitigation. He told the judge all the good points, really most of which she was already aware, as they had been firm friends for so long.

SS nodded as sagely as a stuffed corgi in the back of a rusty Cortina with each word of the mitigation. Then BO sat down, more pleased than Punch at his natural eloquence, at least as he perceived it. All the roaming donkeys in the area struggled without four legs because of his loquacity in talking the hind legs off of most of them.

SS then went through the judicial motions and said, 'Although you have pleaded guilty to a serious offence, there are several points in your favour as your Counsel has so eloquently addressed in mitigation. However it must be marked with a sentence of imprisonment. But as you gave pleaded guilty, have many personal factors in your favour and have never been convicted before, I can suspend the sentence. You will serve a sentence of 2 years' imprisonment suspended for 12 months.

It was all planned in advance behind the scenes in Chambers as the usual legal oil that lubricates the machinery of justice being a nod is better than a wink to a blind horse. Judge SS continued with her other cases. She then adjourned the court until the following day.

Unknown to all except the parties, SS was due to appear before Judge PP the next day. It was to be a repeat performance with their roles in reverse. It was agreed in advance as a routine example of the same legal back-scratching.

During the evening, as there was no work to do given the sentencing was already agreed on the nod, PP started to polish off the odd decanter of red wine. Generally she did not drink much at all because it made her temperament worse. Once she started drinking, she could never stop. That made her more morose than ever. Then she usually got to thinking about a 'life and what's it all about' scenario. It solved nothing except to add to her natural curmudgeonly disposition and suppressed depression.

This night however was different. Something happened that could neither be foreseen nor imagined, yet it immediately changed PP then and there.

After drinking too much PP fell into an uneasy sleep in front of the flickering television screen. About three hours later she woke up and was troubled because her cat, Zogger Dredd, was not on her lap. He was there when she started drinking. He was always there. He clung to her welcome lap as if he was an appendage attached to her huge belly.

PP called out his name again and again. There was no response. PP went upstairs. She looked in every cupboard and under the duvet and all his secret hiding places. Zogger was nowhere to be seen. His disappearance started to swiftly sober PP up. She went into the garden.

Outside the night was as welcome as a woman in a Taliban cabal. Suddenly the sky changed. The poetry of the night descended upon her garden. In that instant the indigo autumn sky released its rumbling rolling thunder and turned blacker than a chimney sweep's brush. The sky cracked and flashed its message above her, shelling the roof and windows with hail and rain and lightning. The lightning cracked and lit the sky as the hard rain continued to fall. Somehow she knew that she and she alone was the cause of something the karma delivered by the rolling thunder. The poetic message was not lost on her.

Then out of nowhere Zogger was at her feet. She picked him up. He felt awkward and heavy. She carried him into the kitchen. She figured she would give him a rare midnight feast. She put him down. She filled up the bowl.

As she did so she heard a strange mewling muted slightly screeching sigh which then ended in silence. She turned and was stopped in her tracks. Zogger was lying on his side in a pool of fresh spreading blood. He had a crossbow arrow running in and out of his body. She was transfixed by his outstretched body. He did not stir. He never stirred again.

She dug a hole. She buried her rescued cat beneath her feet. She had adopted him as a kitten. He was her only true friend in and out of court. She was no longer drunk. Instead she was out of her head witnessing the frozen pain in Zogger's eyes. Until then she had not realised that just two eyes could hold an ocean of tears, made worse as they were hers.

The next day SS appeared before Judge PP. She pleaded 'Guilty'.

SS had the same lawyer, BO, as PP had the previous day. He made similar points in mitigation. He nodded and smiled at the judge. Judge PP returned the nods and smiles with those of her own. It was as perfunctory as they had planned.

At the end BO said, 'That's all I wish to say unless there is any other point I can help Your Honour with?'

'No,' said Judge PP. 'You have said all that could be said. No one could have said more.'

Each of PP and SS and BO acted as if in a professional pantomime for the public who of course had no idea of the background of the defendants and their long term friendship. Equally no one had any idea about the planned expected sentence.

Then PP came to sentence SS. She looked at her and caught her eyes in a sharp focus. PP fixed on her for a while before she even spoke. Then her face changed. Something about the smugness of SS cut her to the quick. Staring at SS she saw an image and felt pangs of sadness about Zogger. She could not shake off the crossbow that pierced Zogger's heart. It now pierced hers too. PP suddenly underwent a metamorphosis in court. She sat in silence for some seconds. She changed and became hard-edged, frowning in maps across her troubled forehead. She then started to deliver her sentence:

'You have committed a serious offence. I am surprised by your Counsel's preposterous submissions, especially I should add, that all the while he did so you have been sitting there with a gormless smug self-satisfied smile on your hubristic face. Yet even now you seem not to understand the seriousness of killing endangered species. I would be failing in my public duty if I failed to send you to prison.' She hesitated and added, 'This is the second case of hunters killing endangered animals in this very court in two days.'

SS was riddled with a surprised confusion. She blurted out, 'Your Honour, I am confused. May I address you?' 'No,' said PP. 'Your Counsel has had the opportunity to do so. You do not seem to understand the seriousness of this case. As I said, let me repeat that this is the second such case in two days.'

PP hesitated so her words would hit home:

'You have the unadulterated audacity to come before this honourable court and claim your actions are a form of conservation as if you are serving endangered species when all you are doing is engaged in an endless chain of arrogant ego-driven violence against our fellow creatures. You arrogate to yourself and your cronies the right to decide which animals will live and which ones will die. Why? Yes, why? So you can massage your impostor driven ego to have an animal's head on your grubby blood-stained wall to impress other unimpressive people that you defend as your friends. Your audacity is surpassed by your mindless need for profit or greed when any animal that lives and breathes is unsafe as long as you and your kind have them in your perverted purblind sight. Your frozen heart-...'

SS blurted out, 'But...-'

'There are no buts.'

SS said, 'If...-'

'There are no ifs. You know you are repaying the nation of gorgeous creatures who are doing no harm with your industrial-scale abuse and torture. The animals are intent to live and graze in harmony with nature until people like you come along and pay an extortionate sum to kill them in cold blood. You are destroying their world and ours. Although in your case, it is not cold but hot blood, as you seem to gain such a thrill in taking an innocent animal's life. Why? And for what? Just so you can boast in your silly little golf club and at the fox hunters ball how you slaughtered an elephant or a lion or mass killing of endangered species. You are a despicable specimen of a supposed human being. It would serve you right if an animal turned on you and gobbled your heart up, although I doubt any animal would have good enough sight to find your non-existent heart.

BO could hold his tongue no longer. He stood up and interrupted saying, 'But my Lord there is a precedent...'

'A precedent?'

'Yes, My Lord.'

'Are you serious? If you are you are quite wrong. Now sit down.'

BO sunk and slunk into his seat.

'Let me make it clear. There is no precedent. You might be referring to the pathetic precedent that was set yesterday where a trophy hunter was treated with undue leniency. That was quite a disgraceful sentence. Indeed that evil defendant should have gone straight to prison, where she belonged. If I had been the judge rest assured that is where she would be right now. However a much more important point is these horrible terrible holidays that these greedy people indulge in for their own riches makes me want to vomit. It also sticks in the craw of the public and society and the law. I will not be a party to such undue leniency. This crime is far too common. As I alluded to, there was another case only yesterday - as you state - but that makes your position worse not better. That is all the more reason your client must be subject to the letter of the law.

BO stood up again and said, 'But My Lord, only yesterday when I ...'

'Please do not interrupt me again, unless you have something to say that is worth hearing. Instead let me tell you what I have in mind. I was thinking of a whole life sentence as after all you took the life of an innocent creature and let us be clear not just one. So many for so long you would need an abacus to count the lives of those you have slaughtered. You boasted and boasted in interviews about the sickening photographs with your fat ugly face and bulging beer belly and huge boot on the throat of a giraffe as if killing a harmless animal was some kind of laugh. Well it is time for you to get real. I will wipe the smile off of your smirking face. Indeed I would be failing in my public duty if I did not send you to prison today. The public are outraged by trophy hunters like you who somehow think you are above the law. Well let me tell you that what Thomas Fuller said in 1733 is still applicable today:

Be you never so high, the law is above you.

To upright citizens in our society, people like you slaughtering innocent animals for your perverted pleasure are a tinpot Hitler or a modern day Putin in another guise. If we allow people like you to be free you would end up killing anything and everything in sight. You trophy hunters are lawless and dangerous. I would be failing in my duty by suspending your sentence. With people such as you, with your proclivity, at large in our society, our community would soon become a jungle. Justice would have no meaning.

So you will go to prison. I have reduced the sentence because you pleaded guilty. Although given the extent of the evidence you presented against yourself you actually had no choice, unlike all the animals you have slaughtered without cause or reason or provocation. You will have time to think about your past and present and future during the next decade. You will go to prison for 10 years. Take her down.'

SS's face was riddled red with anxiety and anguish. She looked paler than a dead undertaker.

'I wish to add one point for the record. Rest assured that anyone who comes before me from now on will get a longer sentence. It will be a proper and proportionate sentence given the nature of this crime and the effect on the public and indeed the world. Now is the time to send a message to these criminals and to honour the memory of Zogger Dredd. A wonderful friend killed by another animal abuser.'

Her voice cracked as she got up and left the courtroom.

In the corridor to her Chambers she stopped, stood and wiped her eyes.

The guard jangled his keys. He grabbed SS by her arm. Her face turned a ghostly pale as she was led down the steps to the jail where she would spend the next decade. A cold cemetery silence engulfed the whole courtroom and the cells. Juggling with his keys while changing hands to grab SS he dropped the bunch which resounded as steel-on-steel. The silence was broken as the keys sudden fall sounded as sharp as a gunshot.

PP was startled by the sound as if she expected to see an elephant drop down dead. As she left the courtroom she missed her step. She stumbled and tumbled and fell. She screamed in pain. She landed awkwardly against the Victorian iron railings. The force of her fall caused a gash to her face. Her legs folded under her. As she fell blood poured from her forehead and onto her face. She landed in a scrunched pile on the broken concrete at the bottom of the shaky stairs leading to her Chambers. A pool of blood spread from her mouth and head.

Hearing her scream, the guard rushed behind the court. Seeing the judge the guard dared not move her lest it caused more medical problems. Everyone scrambled into action. The paramedic called for an ambulance as he rushed through the courtroom. The next sound was an 'emergency' call to the cells below. Within moments they heard the siren sound of the ambulance, faint at first then getting louder as it got closer to the court.

By the time the ambulance arrived PP had not changed her position. She lay in a crumpled heap. The paramedic examined her. He looked at his colleague and gently, almost imperceptibly, nodded his head. His staring eyes told their own story. There was no need for words. There was no rush.

All her life PP found pleasure in causing pain and death to endangered animals. Now, sooner than she ever figured, she would join those who were her former playthings in her favourite pastime crime. She would join them forever in the animal netherworld.

The paramedic checked the time then ticked the box on his sheet. He then ticked the box below it. He handed the sheet to his colleague to countersign it.

He signed it too, noting the time they had arrived. The two signatures confirmed that the patient, formerly an impatient irascible judge, was 'DOA'.

A Woman and a Hat and a Black Cat

Flames licked her feet
Fire burned her limbs
Screaming with confused innocence
Prayer and prejudice were the twins
Mixed as one as the fire flew high
Her soul sold by stone-hearted strangers
Her fortune fixed by biased neighbours
Under a crescent moon and a starless sky

Flames locked her face
Scorched her pale wrinkled skin
Her eyes burned by fiery guilt
Her skeleton cursed by mortal sin
A neighbour cabal saw fit to light a fuse
Beneath her broken body born to lose
Our history with a reason for the Blues
A suspect truth proved as a social ruse

Whatever was a trumped up reason
As always never mattered too much
As long as we could burn another woman
Left without a friend or funds or a crutch
For good measure throw her in a dirt-ridden ditch
No cemetery sermon for a woman branded a witch
So the lies die on her tongue as no truth could tell
We grabbed her broomstick and hat and cat as well
Lest his magnetic green eyes
Would remind us of our lies
No memory of our bias could survive
Her companion cat staked by her side

All's well so our victims could end well
Their future forged when our prejudice fell
Burned and buried in our earthbound hell

The burning glowed from Essex to Salem
A country and century separated them
Discovered its target across tide and time
Find a vulnerable victim to use and condemn
The witch's cat is an ideal victim to abuse
Proves our reason for a raging ruse to use
Other lives we choose as to who will lose
Black defines the woman her cat and her hat
Burned on the anvil of our biased eye-tooth
We need no evidence when we run out of ruth
Our power of prejudice stands the test of time
A power without reason as a substitute for truth

Written in Water

Burn the blue moon so it cries in the sky
Sell our soul while the whole world starts to fry
Chase the last polar bear with blood-lust eyes
Our false valentine of death in disguise

The stream dries and dies before our eyes
Poisoned by all our phoney leaders' lies
Our world plunges towards destiny's cell
For this time the chime strikes our own death knell

Icebergs melt on the horizon
When the heat keeps on rising
The polar bear is caught in our storm's eye
Then hung out to dry
Left to starve and die
Like our lambs we lead to the slaughter
The killing seas begin the flood
While our fate bathes in their blood
Our future is forged and written in water

Red clouds of dust smother our mother earth
Much too late to count the cost of her worth
While our planet is taking its last breath
Our kiss steals her life by our Judas death

In Good Company

Vistal Garg wired his cute barb
Sacking 900 workers over Zoom
He hardly had to leave the room
To make his point and shout about
How they were 'too damn slow'
Adding to his huge financial woe
They were a 'bunch of dumb dolphins'
Lest they missed his point Garg barked
'Dumb dolphins get caught in nets
Dumb dolphins get eaten by sharks'
Loyalty to those who made his fortune
So much money for so many years
Between milking their tears and fears
Garg's problem was he never understood
However much money you have made
It is never any good
To use a victim to make a victim
By a low blow limbo
From a dude well below the grade
Yet it is not hard to fathom
How Garg sells his hokum
You cannot buy wisdom
Or disguise a behemoth ego

Dolphins and people are not dumb
Though one who tries to treat one
For the other
As if they were much like him
Making each worker his victim

Shows we can ignore his gargantuan ego
Whose intellectual incline is pyrrhic
Words as wise as a Guns N' Roses lyric
As for rescuing a drowning Garg
You wonder if a dolphin could be bothered
With someone whose morals are smothered
In the scheme of things you might guess
They would rescue him nevertheless
Unlike Garg dolphins do not charge
Unlike Garg dolphins are quite smart
Unlike Garg dolphins are quite kind
They act according to a sound mind
Balanced by an open thumping heart
Dolphins do not see saving a human
As other than part of their altruistic art
If Garg had a modicum of their attributes
With time even he might end up being cute

Pshaw he said to the Irish

The Irish have good reason to hate the English
Century-upon-century as victims of inhumanity
Soldiers ever-bolder in how they were treated
The bash bosh bish towards the biased English
Plus the wry smile of satisfying their vanity

In 2021 Stormont politicians had the chance
To ban hunting and let compassion advance
Especially as the English had provided a lead
The Irish had a straight aim in an open mind
A chance to prove animal abuse was left behind

Yet the numbers were the crunch of the vote
Seeing hunted animals as a distorted reflection
Of their own limited value by the English
They voted in the ban 38 for and 45 against
When the voiceless were dished by the Irish

GBS said 'pshaw' and he is one who knows
He spoke loudly from an unforgiving grave
His voice more serious than even his life itself
Seeing he knew first-hand all about the English
How animal life would be squandered not saved

The Irish became a sad imitation
Of their forever historical foes
Who put their country on the line
To render a fight or just surrender
Given this in the land of Behan

An echo of the Black and Tans
Against their bright fire and tune
With the rising of the rebel moon
Proving to be political poltroons
The Irish were crass and selfish
Making GBS even more waspish
Less a leprechaun and more elfish
Animal abuse was too hard to relinquish
Equally unequal as too weak to squish
Too tough for those morally vanquished
Proved to be much worse than the English
Shaw sure enough knows the Irish
Dyed in the wool as pale English
Just unjust and gonzo priggish
Lost in a maze of Delphic Gaelic

Meet Me beneath the Magic of our Moon

I never realised that just two eyes
Could hold so many tears
Until I lost you I never knew blue-on-blue
Would force me to reveal my red raw fears

My head and your heart are two worlds apart
With no one I can trust
Every night I'm awake with this ache I can't fake
It's just that I'm lost without your stardust

Without you my feline friend
My world has come to an end
My spirit has turned to rust
My soul seeks the spark of your stardust
Without you the midnight sky has no stars
My mind is chained inside locked lovelorn bars
Without you the night has no moon
My heartstrings are all out of tune
Yet we can read the rhythm of our natural rune
If you meet me beneath the magic of our moon

It is not too late for us to fight fate
See you in a new world
We could be free from the prison of destiny
To find all we lost without your stardust

A Fish Out Of Water

'Fishing is my way of breathing' said Ted Hughes
Casting a line and a lie savouring his views
The poetry of prejudice as his fuse
It is a shame fish do not feel the same
While Hughes may breathe easier with his muse
Using poetry as a talent to abuse
The fish has no one to mourn in the pews
Hughes claimed fish were cold
Putting his conscience on hold
A tale at odds with one Plath told
Checking the corpse he had caught
His crooked hook making her life nought
Hughes gloried in his deathly news
Finding fun in how fish fought to live
Giving him a reason and rhyme for his ruse
A crowd gathered round his bloodied body
A macabre greed greater than any need
A lost lonely fish with nothing left to lose
Easing Hughes troubled heart with speed
Finding solace when a victim pays his dues
When Hughes breathed his last he could use
A certain truth whilst his losing body stews
His breath stops a fish from living
It is a carp he cannot hide
Hughes past proves his breathing
Is a way of life while his victim died
Fishing and wishing as a catch perishes
A slaughter in water of his scum tide
All he seems to have gained from pain
A self-serving pathetic phoney pride
Breathing hubris poetry no boast can hide

Grandma what is a Gorilla

There was a time not so long ago
I could have told you what I know
About our huge hairy foreign friends
Who happened to be happy in the jungle
Living by their own means and ends
Until they became victims of our fungus
When we used machines to make money
By destroying their trees and the honey
Then using all the timber and their land
To make even more money by our plans
So as we still beg and borrow and lift
We try to sell an idea our greed is a gift
A satire we learned from bitter-sweet Swift
Then sent in our own group of guerrillas
Now you ask me 'What is a gorilla?'
I am stumped to find an answer
Our theft of their home environment
Meant no less than our nature's cancer
All we offered was a bulldozer and a gun
We razed all their forests
Then destroyed their freedom
For what then was a gorilla
Cannot be disguised as vanilla
There are so very few left in our world
Their flag of freedom is forever unfurled
Except for a stereotypical view in our zoo
The Swift gift we can use without a trace
No guilt or remorse of any sort in its place
As we forget the feelings with no disgrace

Forget who we killed in our consumer race
For the last time we see their true base

I wish I could tell you something
That is much better than what I can
My quiet hope my dear grandson
Is for a change before you are a man
The gift we had we foolishly destroyed
The gift we see is an image of our void
The gift we give is wrapped cancroids

If you get a chance to see such a species
Grab it with both hands as he is on the list
For if you blink I fear he will disappear
As the last gorilla in the fading mist

A Green River Killer Revisited

The advance of a rudderless ship
With no one competent at the tiller
Every child can become the President
Yet misreading the legal crumbling pillar
Leads to a crass view of their Constitution
So every creep can become a serial killer
By misinterpreting the 'right to bear arms'
As a perverse solecistic legal prostitution

Yet rest assured as with our American cousins
England breeds creeps by the sixes and dozens
Ian Brady had a heart of grimy granite
When it came to killing he would pan it
To sift a victim according to his whim
His favourite was climbing to a top flat
Then find another trusting purring cat
Then fling the creature through the air
Laughing as like the last one she went splat
Sprawled dead in blood on a 'Welcome' mat
Until he found someone better than that
A friendly trusting child as a substitute cat
When Brady started his plan to torture children
He had the benefit of the warped Myra Hindley
She matched and surpassed his penchant for killing
Starting with poison and strangling hungry pigeons
Waiting for the one who was eager to feed them
They soon found out her fondness to seed them
When they died before her eyes she just juggled
A love for their pain she indulged in again and again

Together Brady and Hindley became a killing duo
A hatred of children burned bright day and night
Catching the disease of conceit to feed their might
No difference between an animal and a child
All that mattered was their victims
Were vulnerable and could be defiled
What really set them alight
So each could sew and grow
Their rancid seed of killing children
Made each other's savage heart thrive
Half-satisfied when few were left alive
Feeding their intent as a killers' bent

From Bundy to Dahmer and Ridgway to Spencer
Each used a different method yet no less tenser
All had the same aim to find someone alone
Offer a lift or a gift or a bed in their home
Where between being an animal
Or a passing defenceless stranger
Was the same to each criminal
Presenting an ever pressing danger
Each in their own way just another clone
A life route and death chosen as an offshoot
Their rotten fruit was just the same
When it came to burying the bones
Finding someone weak and random to kill
An animal or a child was grist to their mill

When the scales are balanced with weight
The sordid saga of killers heavy with hate
Torturing children and animals

As fully-fledged inbred criminals
Death-smells filter through fear and sheer terror
When any life ends by a knife or in an abattoir
A fact that hits with an immediate impact
Without an excuse or escape from the truth

Huntley was the same as the rest
His aim to use strength to wrest
The lifeblood from two young schoolgirls
Intending to destroy their whole world
A pervert ever alert as to who he could hurt
Animals and children were his two targets
Gaining a killer's skill with an evil swipe
His practice followed the mass-archetype
A vulnerable victim's life one to be wiped

However harsh one we cannot avoid or ignore
As their cruelty strikes our humanity's core
Serial killers who murdered on the loose
Became an artisan and craftsman criminal
Honing their heart moving from hand to eye
Trading every life for a lie upon a lie
First practised their skill on animal-after-animal

The Blackboard Jungle

The teacher told the class
About Darwin and the mass
Of creatures he discovered
Who were in so many ways like us
Existing to survive no less than Dreyfus
It was a lesson worth learning
Experiments of our yearning
Information we gain from vivisection
With no harm to us and no objection
Their pain our gain to remain sane
Said the teacher as he explained
How we have won by a self-selection
When a boy at the back of the class
Who rarely asked a single question
And if asked answered 'pass'
Who everyone branded a dunce
Because of what he did once
When he was very young
Thereafter soiled and spoiled by bias
Raised his hand and shyly asked:
'Sir, if they are the same as us
Why do we treat them as such rubbish
Just to use and abuse and put them in zoos?'
The teacher prepared a set text to spout
To prove the boy was typically confused
With no idea what he was asking about
Characteristically based on his intellect
In turn based on a 'C' stream selection
It would not be hard to fool him

With benefits we gain from vivisection
The child became tongue-tied and silent
While he waited for the teacher to mumble
When the bell rang to end the life lesson
Leaving the question in dusty fading chalk
Where logic and lies take a literary tumble
As the noisy class left the blackboard jungle

A Procrustean Apology

All say 'sorry' as if a politician's plea
Meaning I hope you'll feel sorry for me
For where principle counts for nothing
All lies can be sold and bought
I would not have dreamed of uttering
Some useless or pointless apology
Except for the fact that 'I was caught'

Could be that fat creep Elliott
Who laughed drain-style of course
Sitting astride a sad-eyed laid-out horse
Who could not move a muscle or his head
The obese creep knew she was already dead

Mickey Todd was an abusive sod
Who whipped and whipped a horse
With branches he grabbed in a temper
Struck the horse who faltered at the water
Todd did not care as it was only a horse
Who had in her time won him slight fame
And even a good name at least until now
As day becomes night he became a knight
As any other politician who dishes the dirt
Not caring who or why someone was hurt
Unless he hit her in a tempered curse
A victim who could not resist such force
Ideally a frightened spooked whipped horse

At Madox Farm workers caught on camera

Bullying pride they did not even try to hide
A Zouma kick to a cow in the belly and chest
They raised another by a hoist from her rest
Then smacked one in the face with a spade
Because the cow was too scared to move
Though who and why of those were savage
Was plain to see it is these farm workers
Who could be you or worse or all of us

Forget the foolish plea to forget
The animals and just 'move on'
That is no answer at all then or now
To the abused cat or horse or cow
Who might now be dead and gone

With the sincerity of a politician
They make a pointless repetition
They stretch their Procrustean bed
Robber liars whose muddled head
In and out of Parliament is spent
Finding excuses then twisted and bent
Selling us a second-rate insincerity
To try to fool the public and society
They offer deception that is never bought
We know their delivery adds up to nought
Abuse by bullies and cowards is self-taught
Never ever apologising for their onslaught
From the camera and letter and tape
Moving every which way to find an escape
However dressed up the words always sought
Hide that they mean 'I'm sorry I was caught'

Paulo the Pussyfooter

In the blackness of night
He was right out of sight
Paulo scaled the drainpipe
He was greeted by a scene
Reflecting a moon in his happy face
There on the line was the frilly lace
Scrambled across the line for an ace

Dancing as a squirrel not a cat
He brought it down on the grass
Held the lace between his teeth
The bra dangled as a saxophone
He swiftly snatched it fancy that
As if he was a dog with a bone
Balancing as a high-wire cat
Paulo scarpered to safety racing home

The next day he wandered afar
Peering into the darkest garden
Past the priest's early morn sermon
Before the lady's pants were missed
Hidden by the fast fading grey mist
Before her last secret partner's kiss
Paulo brought her the pink lacy pants
His owner was somewhat taken aback
She looked at Paulo somewhat askance
'You're a badass cat that's for sure'
Half-smiled for he touched her core

Until that is the next dark night
When Paulo lit out at midnight
As usual he was up to no good
Prowling in the neighbourhood
Paulo chanced upon a hip group
Listening entranced to a music loop
Followed by an odd holler and a hoop
As they smoked Paulo quietly snooped
Hiding in the shadows ready to swoop

Laying out flat as the music played
Paulo had no reason to be afraid
Amused he caught a pipe in his paw
Juggled and hooked the tobacco too
Which the group covertly grew
Paulo's act was perhaps a bit rash
As he had grabbed their secret stash
Pure punk skunk was high value cash

Yet no longer as a passing stranger
Pussyfoot Paulo relished the danger
Paulo never stayed for very long
Before the strain of the last song
Paulo was already up and gone
He swiftly returned to his mistress
Getting back to where he belonged
Flying fast with the wind
In a night-time heady pong
His head was spinning with a winning song
Clenched teeth clasped a classic brass bong

In their rancid hearts and jammed moral cogs
Along with black people they hanged 4000 dogs
Alas victims were dismissed with common sass
Nameless in a redneck circus as a lynched carcass
A name signifies an identity in society
So no need of a name for an animal slave
Framed to be a number by you and me
Whose death is all that sets them free

Scapegoats towards Slaughter

They line up ready
In an orderly queue
Into a death-swelling transporter
Denied a last meal
No reason to waste water
Noses out of wooden slats
To breathe before the splat
Eternal scapegoats for slaughter

In hunched pain together
In an orderly queue
Idly whacked by bloody sticks
By bored spattered workers
Arriving at a dark backwater
Their impatience caught her
With no time for any shirkers
Eternal scapegoats for slaughter

They line up ready
In an orderly queue
Forced to emit their last snorter
Then tipped upside down
Their throats slit amid a pumped aorta
A ritual religion bought her
A dying fixed face frown
Eternal scapegoats for slaughter

No more orderly queue
No one to support her

Our profits rise above water
With each drowned animal
Eternal scapegoats for slaughter
The plimsoll line of suffering
As every animals' offering
We borrowed from religion
A scapegoat and a stool-pigeon
Blaming animals for our acts
Escaping evidence and facts
Use trite wisdom as a sapient saw
Relying on religion as hard law
Eye-for-eye except it is easy to defy
If you do not need to see eye-to-eye
Moreover neither is it tooth-for-tooth
For how can a carcass decry the truth?

When it comes to killing a stranger
If it is someone who is not your kind
Another species is seen as a money-changer
We use a Nelsonian eye to feign being blind

DNA of a Politician

Rees-Mogg asked Reg Presley
If he could join The Troggs
Reg was far too shrewd
He knew Mogg was no dude
When he backed foie gras
To satisfy his Somerset mates
Then backed the new GM
To kill any thoughts of ALM
Breeding animals resistant to disease
So farmers would gain higher profits
While animals would be caught off it
By breeding solely female chickens
So no male eggs were despatched
While share holders kept finger-licking
The gain from it did not escape old Mogg
Who was always something of a clever dog
When it came to making an unhealthy profit
Would hold and unfold a clenched fist
Figured it could be a new miracle-drug
A reverse kind of vivisection on a mind
Taking the tablet day after day in earnest
Might be a future once believed impossible
Einstein meets the bride of Frankenstein
To discover a new form of fire as Prometheus
Doomed to failure as nature's gaoler
Saw the definition of a politician as 'a liar'
Parliament a place where every face wore
A sphincter smile hiding their pants on fire
All doubt removed and resolved by a nudist
An experiment in belief to change an atheist
An experiment doomed to fail its purpose
An experiment to make a politician honest

Robots Never Bleed

The metal detector vivisectionist
Bent over the nameless exhibit
Stretched by a strap in a steel trap
Unable to resist the gibbet
The only sound to be heard
An echoed rattle without a word
From the exhibit's clamped teeth
Fixed in fear with a forced grin
Waiting for the end of the pain
Waiting in pain in vain again
Waiting for no reason but to die

A vivisectionist held the moving tool
A tool twisting and turning on a tool
The metal scarred the exhibit
Whose voice-box was removed
She mimicked e mimicked a goldfish howl
A fear-filled face without a growl
Probed from her heart to her bowel
Advances are red-hot
The scientist is a robot
The robot only rusts
The animal bleeds and dies
Then returns to ashes and dust
Her tool took the tool's life
A plight forfeited by our right
To plunder and rent asunder

Those fed our drugs to die
Scared mongrels lined up to fry
Four and twenty pigeons in a pie
The needle nails our every lie
As science serves to paralyse
Animal exhibits their scapegoat prize
Another death not worth a sigh
A new scientist no one could defy
A new scientist no emotion to deny
A new scientist whose circuits lie
Yet spills no tears or blood
A death with no reason to decry
Robots neither bleed nor cry

Time-bomb Heart

It's a beautiful day
Let's go out and destroy something

There's a blood-red sky kissed by a passing wispy cloud
Blood on the lips of the circling hungry vulture crowd
Death on the teeth of the unleashed invading hound
Blood in the bubble that traps her pleading crying voice
Death on the blade that destroys his future crushed choice
Blood on her forehead is the child's forever losing prize
Death on our hands after the first Kremlin bullet flies
Blood in the mind of the Russki's manufactured lies
Death on the tongue of Putin while he tries to paralyse
Blood on the sword of Islam serving to cannibalise
Death in the word of the Taliban seeking to terrorise
Matching the fear-filled light doused in freedom's
   dying eyes

It's a beautiful day
Let's go out and murder truth

A Pope and a Pet

The Pope sermonizing for our redemption
Claimed 'couples who choose to forego
Children and prefer pets are selfish'
Perhaps why religion abhors angelfish
For he should know as one in the know
Who subscribes to the story of a starfish
Is an admission no need to parry a priest
In a religion whose priests do not procreate
Though they are happy to orally vibrate
Renaming parenthood he claimed
'Takes away your humanity'
Failing to see what promotes poverty
On a tightrope balanced by missal inanity
Between profundity and priest-led profanity
His no dope-false hope of an idea
Springs from a notion of Vatican vanity

His religion is focused on a falsehood foxhole
Only humans matter as only humans have a soul
From half-baked ideas of Aristotle
All were void and devoid of bottle
To a prejudiced virus honed by Aquinas
A theory based on an idea with a hollow whole
Perfect progress to drag religion into the 21st century
Adopting a rescued cat or dog or any stray animal
Would show the meaning of common humanity
Perhaps if he helped any abandoned animal to cope
Maybe the Pope would be practising Christianity

In his vast wealthy world in the richest place
The Pope fails to find a welcome space
For the homeless and the abused children
As well as our countless abused animals
Whose lives have all been unfurled
While he parades in his privileged world
They seek nothing more than a passion
Of humility and a mite from St Francis
Delivering the kissed riches of compassion

Priests without children with evil intent
Are content to loiter outside the tent
Then hide behind the beguiled smile
Of the prancing practised paedophile
It is little wonder lest he forgets
A reason some people prefer pets
Rather than stare into his religious abyss
How much wiser he would prove to be
Following the teaching of St Francis
Who saw the church as cause and effect
Of so much avoidable animal misery
Spreading his message wider than Assisi
So much better than another red letter
From the privileged poise of one who can
Find odd succour behind the gilded walls
Where valuable paintings hang in the halls
No eyes see the battered homeless woman
No thoughts given to the forgotten tarpan

Christian Brothers and nuns in Ireland
Abused the children because they could

Killed the baby and destroyed the mother
To a woman and a man because they can
Then in Canada for over 100 years
Truth grabbed at birth and smothered
The Pope visits to offer a pious apology
To the Indians enslaved at five-years-old
The abused in mind and body and heart
By religious zealots ripping them apart
Hearing they were no different than a buffalo
Added another kind of abuse to their woe
When the Chiefs heard his words 'I apologise'
They recognised the impact of imported lies

A starving dog barks at the departing caravan
A poverty of morality forced by one who can
Imposed on the universe by one in the Vatican
Pius XII agreed with Hitler to hide the priests
Who abused children and then fled to the East
Meanwhile today another choirboy is defiled
Hidden from the public and any prying eyes
Priest perverts abuse another defenceless child
The problem is so near and yet so clear
Could be seen by any passing blind beggar
In a skip-rescued broken Vatican mirror

Jews Don't Count

With or without an axe many claim
Jews are abused by those who choose
To rebuke them and malign them
Without any reason at all
Except it is just part of the system
That fails to control them
Since being banished by the English
In the 12th century by our pious bias

Yet abusing animals does not count
In any degree or calculated amount
A truth Jews still have to surmount

Jews are prone to being prejudiced
For no reason except they are Jews
They deserve to be treated with justice
Which is the same as most of us want too
Yet it seems strange that when there were
6 million Jews killed in Hitler's camps
Perhaps they would not want other creatures
Ritually abused when their cramped lives end
90 million animals are slaughtered each year
To satisfy the religious rites they demand
Causing suffering animals even more suffering

Prejudice against animals by Jews echoes
Muslims who choose animals as victims too
So as a religion dictum that claims
Jews Don't Count with the Muslims
Shows neither of them count animals at all
The mathematics of the religious calculus

A trigonometry of prejudice by them and us
The unanswered question serves to perplex
Using algebraic custom to claim immunity
Visiting the consequences with impunity
Given prejudice on prejudice by faith and skin
Proving animals do not count in their religion

Yet have Jews and Muslims considered
Why animals do not count for them at all
Or is it that their rites mean they must fall
Their suffering is not even worthy of a call
A religion based on prejudice has a lot of gall
So that some might well wish to question
The division between ethics and complexion
A religion with self-created self-serving ideals
Might not balance how a non-believer feels
Getting worked up because Jews Don't Count
Stings the choice between abuse and suffering
Might be displaced when suffering is paramount

Then again the Uighurs are victimised
As can be expected by the biased Chinese
Who want them to see with Chinese eyes
Even if Jews Don't Count in any amount
It is tantamount to seeing a catamount
As an omen for a time from history's Fall
Animals count for nothing in their religion
As with so many can count for nothing at all

So save your repeated bleat
Until you are ready to quit gorging meat
A truth written in water is plain to see

To cause ritual slaughter offends society
When prejudice is proved and removed
Yet solved by the Jewish Vegetarian Society
Muslims too can be free in the same degree
By joining the Muslim Vegetarian Society
Can they remove the scales of injustice
Or are we too blindsided to see
Blindfolded to the abattoir's misery
How you can claim it is wrong all along
To be a victim of prejudice without cause
Then practice prejudice on dying animals
Relying on a belief borne of religious laws
Might give Jews and Muslims cause to pause

Religion is their religion
No one else can build a bridge on
Yet religion is only religion
When truth is avoided as a smidgen
Then add to an animal's suffering
When denial should replace prayer
As death waits inside the gates of an abattoir
There remains the clincher and stinger
From a worthy Nobel Prize Winner
The redoubtable Isaac Bashevis Singer
A Jew who knew what was true:
There is only one little step from killing animals
To creating gas chambers a la Hitler and
Concentration camps a la Stalin...all such deeds
Are done in the name of "social justice".
There will be no justice as long as a man will stand
with a knife or with a gun and destroy those who are
weaker than he is.

Syphilis in Tuskegee

Their conspiracy cabal thrived
Infected victims and their wives
The children lost their lives
Others disabled and born blind
Died in agony before their time
A sign proved the one-line track
The doctors to a man were white
While every single victim was black

Nazis formed their intent from the start
Smashing each Jewish mind and heart
Denying them any comfort or a bed
Standing huddled in a railway shed
Transported when they ran out of luck
Freighted women and children and men
Day and night packed tight in cattle trucks
Awaiting fate by a visit from Death's Angel
In the shape of a butcher-vivisector Mengele

Doctor Sims in Tuskegee never met Mengele
The vivisector-butcher had never heard of Sims
Yet the two doctors shared a cruel common craft
Each one had practised their profession on animals
Graduated to be charlatan craftsman criminals
Each seduced by power over powerless as their key
A guarantee no one in their grasp would ever be free
Vulnerable wounded and wasted to die without liberty
There was no reason for scientists to stick with animals
When with ease they could experiment on you and me

In England the ideas filtered into Porton Down
Where those standing up were soon put down
War was the reason the soldiers were in pain
War was the reason pigs were put in the frame
Their skin was so close to soldiers using a gun
Who were wounded heroes hit by an enemy gun
Shot in battle with their life and death on the run
Now the pigs too had run out of luck
Each pig looked at the cocked rifles
As they had seen the scientist as a friend
Until their echoing squeals were stifled
A repeat bullet-round signalled each pig's end

Some were penniless
All were powerless
No selection between a sinner and a saint
Prejudice unleashed was without restraint
Once grasped by every medical Nazi asp
No one could ever be free
Every doctor delivered the dosed disease
Law and morality lost in a deep-freeze
Slaughter of the innocents by syphilis in Tuskegee
400 men for 40 years tortured by science immorality

Now is not the time to shake a head and mutter tut
There never was and never is a reason to pussyfoot
Yet let us not seek our reason to only condemn them
For animals their per diem at our hands is their requiem

Black is the Colour

Agnes Waterhouse was feared by neighbours
Attacked as anti-social in her labours
Keeping herself-to-herself they levelled at her
As a crime when all she wanted was no favours
Happy to live on her own terms
Agnes stood firm and never squirmed
Agnes was her own woman
Agnes was made of tough stuff
Agnes refused to turn for the worms
The neighbours burned her to death
Then to be sure they found 500 more
So their black arts soul would be rived
Before fully burned they were cut down
One by one they were buried alive
So a single woman would not survive

Agnes had few friends and no funds
A community of cautious black cats
A couple who wore pointed black hats

Villagers had free rein to practise prejudice
For the biased cynics their pain cut no ice
Agnes and her black cat were burned in a pack
The rest was a smokescreen and a smokestack
Then thrown together into the freshly dug pit
Using joint hate as their neighbourly template
Screeching bodies of the squirming black cats
Fighting death as the soil covered their noses
The Essex people went about their business

Tending graves with sweet smelling pink roses
Marking the graves of the ones who died
People's prejudice burned bright with pride

A woman screamed yet no one heard her
A woman against neighbours who hurt her
A black cat against the ones who burnt her
A woman with a black cat meets prejudice
A woman with reason enough for all of us
A woman and cat condemned due to colour
A woman and a cat hanged by the jugular
A woman with a black cat without purdah
A woman worthy of our past resort to murder
A woman alone is a target for a cop to murder

An animal and a woman without a girder
Has no protection from those who herd her
Abusers use a victim as a slur for their spur
After 400 years they view Agnes and her cat
Through the same skewed vision of a voyeur

A Creed of Claudette Colvin

Fired by her baptism
She was caught between
Fighting the face of racism
Or a climb-down surrender
That could bend and break her
On a cold day in March 1955
Her spirit truly came alive
She would not take a dive
Claudette Colvin at just 15
She was born with a rebel mind
She was no white man's slave
She was no black man's pet
She was 100% her own girl
The world would find out yet

Sitting with three friends on the bus
The white driver told them to move
Without causing any kind of fuss
Move to the back as is your place
Any black face in the white space
Struck a cuss in the driver's craw
To see any black and any squaw
All in all it was an instant williwaw
Claudette knew it was against the law

Claudette was caught in a legal trap
Her mind was a mixed-up moral map
Saying 'sorry' and then forced to move
What could or would it serve or prove

She might move an Uncle Tom in town
Or should she stay standing up
Fighting for her rights by sitting down
A time when her life ran out of rhyme
Colvin was no puppet or clown
Colvin's concern did not linger
Staring at the driver's pointed finger
She was ready to sing her own song
She knew in her heart what was right
She knew in her soul he was wrong
Her friend A moved to the back
Her friend B feared arrest too
Holding their heads low slunk away
C feared arrest too if she stayed
She did not intend to offend
So she too scurried to the back
Where the seats were reserved
For people deemed to be inferior
Unlike whites born to be superior
Unlike blacks as a passing plasma
For people deemed black anathema
All in all no different than animals
Her friends sat behind the white folks
While her ire was poked and stoked
Claudette sat on the bus in the front
In downtown Montgomery Alabama
The lesson learned at her mother's knee
Circled her mind knowing she was free
Told by her Mama every day in every way
'Listen, you may be born with black skin
But Honey you're as good as all of them

No better, but you sure ain't no worse
Let me tell you being black ain't a curse'

Colvin steeled herself and sat tight
As always she was ready for a fight
Knowing her old Mama was right
She stared dead-eyed at the driver
Her flint face reflecting life's race
Straight into his white glinting face
She stayed sitting tight in her space
She said so others heard her case
'I paid for a seat I ain't going to go
To the back where blacks are on show
You'd better know I am not your negro'

Claudette knew if she moved to the back
It would be an act she would forever regret
Claudette was no white or black man's pet

On one shoulder she had Harriet Tubman
On the other she had Sojourner Truth
On the thundering Underground Railroad
She saw each ghost of justice as an omen
Claiming to the world 'Ain't I a Woman'

Colvin stayed in her seat
Colvin planted her feet
Until without seeking favour or fuss
She was dragged right off the bus
Two burly cops and almost concussed
Handcuffed and taken to the jailhouse

Locked in a cell so the past criminals
Left her overcome by the stale smell
Deprived even of a mattress and sleep
Her head started to swim and swell
She thought about 'heaven and hell'
To teach her a lesson to remember
She was denied a blanket and food
She was a target for pointed insults
Crass and crude and racist and rude
Practised insults blunt and sharp
Revolved inside her head
Lewd and intended to intrude
Yet for her their words did not count
Their swaggering mood and attitude
Sweaty jailers with nothing to prove
Locked inside their own false pride
Born of a congenital societal groove
All her companions moved giddy-up
Now was not the time to fit or quit
She stayed sitting as the face of injustice
Supped her freedom from a broken cup

Thrown off and under their bus
A stance that made her dance
Yet for her it was ever thus
So every black voice could sing
Flying with Colvin's freedom wing

The driver saw her as one
Only fit to sit at the back
Or on the stained floor

So the smell of a cell
Was similar to an abattoir
They sought to destroy her mind
Yet Claudette had such insight
She saw truth and law were blind
She knew she was not a criminal
She knew if you were born black
It was an everyday gimcrack
Or worse were born an animal
Stalked as if you were a humpback
Open prejudice was never subliminal
When you were caught in the trammel

The cops and jailers failed in the end
Well-deserved in the way life wends
In 2021 Colvin's conviction was quashed
Her stance on injustice now runs free
It is time to rejoice in her choice
Declared innocent at the age of 88
Her voice reverberates in world history
Her voice unlocked what it is to be free
When the good and bad flashes
When the right and wrong clashes
Each one has to decide
Which side you are on
Whether you are weak or strong
Are you one more silent coward
Yellow-belly colour of custard
Or will you sing with force
Until you are almost hoarse
A rebel yell to match the boys of Wexford

Singing loud and long your voice as strong
As the rebellion in Claudette Colvin's song
Taught Rosa Parks to take a rebel stance
Taught Martin Luther King to hold a lance
Taught the redneck racists her rebel dance
Taught the Klan that they had no chance
An echo of her stance as a life-long hellion
Resisting the chains of anyone's dominion
Her spirit in a 21st century animal rebellion
Her chimes of freedom are forever rung
For those born to die in agony too young
Sing for those who are forever hamstrung
By being born without a human tongue

How Can a Man be another's Man's Dog
***R v Somerset* [1772]**

James Somerset escaped from his owner
Captured by Charles Stewart on the run
As a hobo on the loose or a stray dog
Much as a slave hiding under a log
Ended up being tried in the High Court
A trial to decide his fate
Money was the prize for the slaver
Somerset stood to lose his liberty
In truth he stood to lose his life
It has no value if a man is never free

Counsel for the slaver said
Somerset is his 'property'
He owns him as he owns his house
As he owns his horse as part of his purse
The judge was prepared to deliver
The slave to be sold down the river
English law made a slave a '*thing*'
The same value as a caged canary
Or a bull with a rusty nose ring
Each his property no less than his life
Just as he owned his servant and wife

Lightning cracked across the sky courtroom
Counsel asked a question jamming legal cogs:
Upon what principle can it ever be an apologue
That a man can become a dog for another man?
In a sentence he declared all the law should ban

Lord Mansfield sucked in his judicial breath
Mulled over matters of law and life and death
Mused on ideas revolving in his confused head
Knowing his judgment would last beyond his time
Rebound long after his toll bell chimed
Wisely he reserved his judgment to be sure
Knowing he could unlock an injustice door
Mansfield figured now and then and forever
Law's free river could never be dammed
By a false claim in his juristic name
Lest law itself would be forever damned

So Mansfield decided once and for all
Fiat justitia, ruat coelum
The Latin phrase did not hide
All that Mansfield had to decide
The balance between freedom and slavery
Scales balancing English law against liberty
A truth that meant he would not hide
When he heard Magna Carta's 1215 credo call:
Let justice be done though the heavens may fall

The cutting question left him agog
Mansfield knew as anyone anywhere
A man could not be another man's dog
No less than a cat or hedgehog or tautog
Or a '*thing*' such as a bog or clog or log
As each struck within Mansfield's reach
His thoughts clawed through a legal fog
When he shot the bolt of his judgment

At once he meant slavery was almost spent:
Slavery is so odious that it must be construed strictly:

> *The air of England has long been too pure for a*
> *slave, and every man who breathes it becomes*
> *free. Every man who comes into this island is*
> *entitled to the protection of English law, whatever*
> *oppression he may have heretofore suffered, and*
> *whatever may be the colour of his skin...Let the*
> *black be discharged.*

Mansfield saw Somerset as someone
Who like him could be and see and feel
The judge first stood in Somerset's shoes
Then stepped inside every black man's shoes
Knowing the reason for his Jim Crow Blues
He knew a black man could never be a thing
He knew if he was wrong the law would lose
He knew Dido his black maid could not choose
He knew their future was much too loose to lose

Law still vibrates with a hollow counterfeit ring
Unlit and until and unless the jungle judge justice
Is satisfied when an animal is born and dies free
No less than a slave was seen to be an entity
With all that freedom can bring
As law is the currency of truth
As law is the currency of blood
We must declare in a jurisprudential flood
An animal is not a legal thing
An animal is entitled to breathe

The English air no less than the King
Their birth and blood is their mainspring
In 2022 a judge must have the sapience
To say today what sentience must bring

An American Judge Jenny Rivera
Said in the New York Court of Appeals
What no one but a judge could deny:
A gilded cage is still a cage
While that has taken until 2022
Law is not law that recoils
From fear to lance the boil
Saying what is and always was true
Now is not the time for us to shrink
An ocean notion of Pythagoras and Leonardo
Whose wisdom on thoughts of freedom
Is the quintessence of our kinship problem
When an animal breathes the air of England
It is to pure for the odious stench of slavery
The soul of the law is written with freedom
Intertwined with the sinews of solid liberty
In mind and heart to let the animal go free
Habeas Corpus should water the truth tree
Change happens at the speed of trust
Yet animals in law are based on human lust
Law is not law that chooses to use a word
Every judge in every court knows is absurd
Bending truth out of shape to suit our world
So nonsensical it has a counterfeit coin ring
An animal is not and never could be a thing

We Can See the Sea

The whale is already fetid
Her tail as rancid and stale
As a politician's promise to be honest
As the impossible is hard to achieve
Once we had a reason to believe
Now somehow fading away we see
While more cling to a sweet ideal
The left and right day and night
Will be alright
As long as we can see the sea

The shark has lost his fins
His tail as rancid and stale
As a predator's promise to shed malice
For a future only a seer could foresee
The daytime darkness raises a plea
Forcing us to realise but still see
While more cling to a sweet ideal
The left and right day and night
Will be alright
As long as we can see the sea

Seals have shed their mottled skin
As if they were pleading volunteers
Neither seeking to resist or prohibit
Ocean research by a Japanese scientist
When anyone asks about anything
Of anyone any time of day you see
While more cling to a sweet ideal

The left and right day and night
Will be alright
As long as we can see the sea

The alligator has snapped his chain
Hose-washed blood erased his name
Along with our memory and his pain
As the claim for a stylish handbag
Is our sole promise that now remain
A search-party sold his life we see
While more cling to a sweet ideal
The left and right day and night
Will be alright
As long as we can see the sea

The crocodile has lost her smile
Drowned in her own forced tears
A blunt knife pierces her wary eye
Seasick sailors search for a lullaby
When she lost her life in sheer fear
Her body pulled by the boat you see
While more cling to a sweet ideal
The left and right day and night
Will be alright
As long as we can see the sea

Dolphin numbers have shrunk
Most lost in a sky blue funk
The scale of the tale they can tell
A stench of a rigour mortis smell
Time for us and them is long gone

Reflecting on our passing we see
While more cling to a sweet ideal
The left and right day and night
Will be alright
As long as we can see the sea

Lobsters changed from pink to black
After a maven armed Spanish attack
Halted breath with limbs idly hacked
The sailors played on any living prey
Passing time towards a judgement day
So there was no way back you see
While more cling to a sweet ideal
The left and right day and night
Will be alright
As long as we can see the sea

Oysters lost their survival shell
When they were all pulverised
By forces from a man-made hell
No rocking at the base of the sea
They grew respected and protected
Until we stole their home you see
While more cling to a sweet ideal
The left and right day and night
Will be alright
As long as we can see the sea

All we can see is the bed of the sea
A rust-riddled floor barely visible
A bed stripped bare yet indivisible

No water now no water anywhere
Salt has turned brooding and dark
The seal has somehow lost her bark
A stark mark hidden from you and me
Blind as we are to our guiding star
For what we see is what we cannot see
We are what we figured we would never be
The land has lost her last torched tree
The sky cries her sad secret silence
For the last uncaged blue-bird
For the free lonely spoiled sea
Kissed by the lonesome land
Reaching out for any true hand
From the sparked lightning stars
Locked behind our human bars
While all the waters burn
Frames our failure to learn
A lesson lifeline of our lifetime
As the last dolphin sighs then dies
Before her intended rightful time

A drooped head of a dying swan
Found a bed she never wanted
Seeped in pools of spreading red
A sleep of the long-time dead
Yet the cataracts of our poison
Tethered to the end of our rope
We face figures we cannot see
Even with a magnified telescope
Less than abandon a sweet ideal
There is a loss of our hope you see

The left and right day and night
Will never be alright
It is not in our sight
For now it can never be

We only listen to self-serving alibis
As a shuttered camera snaps our lies
Willing to be blinded by blurred eyes
We have no need of a clairvoyant
When we can still be nonchalant
Our future forged on a sour spree
A fog-brained present for you and me
We see a fogged future for you and me
The periscope's view is now destroyed
Without any dressed-up excuse or ploy
There is no reason we can be buoyed
Now we can no longer see the sea

Colston's Chains of Change

Colston paraded lies for 125 years
Neither eye washed a single tear
Without sight to see his wraith fear
Selling a coffle by checking shekels
Iron chains on bodies bound naked
Shot through with his putrid hatred

An executioner whose wounds never healed
Colston counted on his contaminated ideals
As those inside the bowels of his ships
Drowned or flayed alive by his whips
His vision seeing people as freight
A bent slaver who was never straight

No longer immune in 2020 on 7 June
Under a red sky lighting a purple moon
Leaving the links of Colston's remains
As the stale stench of a slaver's mange
A dead soul sank in the harbour sea
A dead statue for his musty memory

No force could ever hold you or me
Or anyone who is ever born to be free
But his biased profit from their misery
Dying to breathe Bristol air floating free
Their birthright of natural-born liberty
Chains of change from his prison destiny

Now is not the time to avoid the sting
Knowing a slave was legally a thing
As truth took flight on freedom's wing
Humans legally a quasi-animal 'thing'
Scarred bodies made the slavers sing
Gold a reward slaves' blood would bring

Even in a grave you cannot escape truth
Freedom's flag flew high by the Colston 4
In the splendour of Bristol Crown Court

Roots spread worldwide from our justice tree
A wise jury verdict that set the Colston 4 free
A pulse of justice beats time in the key '*Not Guilty*'

BLM means being free of a nemesis
ALM means being free as a genesis
People and animals used as an alibi
A distorted trope of our historic lies
In the fast-flowing river of never-ending ruth
Animals deserve the same verdict of raw truth
Animals' Lives Matter is one we know forsooth

I Swear I'll Kill It

You see my Bro and me
Well it gave us such a kick
To catch that fear-filled cat
Indulge in a bit of slapstick
Man it was such a crack a hoot
Catching that cute frit furry brute
Grabbing her guts to put in the boot
Then I tell you the best bit of all
Was when she could hardly crawl
When she was trying to escape
From my huge flailing shoes
Another kick and another bruise
I chased her until she was exhausted
She was scared and tired and weary
We laughed so hard we were teary
All the time our laughter chimed
So long and loud we couldn't wait
To share our fun with the crowd
Then at the end of the chase
She was trapped by my young child
Man I tell you Bro it was wild
When she was caught in our trap
I finished her off in seconds flat
By a repeated slap-upon-slap
A perfect ending of my chase
Smack and thwack and whack
Across her bloody unsmiling face
So we put it all out on social media
We wanted to share it with the world
We hurled our fun across the world

What we get up to in our party tricks
It was such a rush to get our kicks
Our new way to travel on Route 66
As the camera captured our laughter
Hell I tell you it was such a thrill
We laughed so it rocked the rafters
To see that manky Bengal cat
Lying helpless on the stained mat
While the camera continued to whirr
We laughed and laughed at her
My Bro and me seeing her misery
Our sour mockery of her heavy purr

A cat's value as one with no soul
Just like the cargo on *The Zong*
Yet they all knew it was wrong
Every game has a loss and a gain
Where a desert is due for the hurt
By Zouma and his cowardly Bro
Measured by a screeching cat's pain

A simple way to assuage
The violence of Zouma's rage
A Judge can put Zouma in a cage
Together with a starving lion
Whose lips are licked and licked
Zouma's pain is not worth a candle
In truth it ain't even worth the wick
As he disappears down the lion's throat
As a natural-born tasty drumstick

If you want to be a hero it is easily done
You just pick anyone vulnerable and weak
Then wreak your bullying violent streak
Find an animal that trusts you
You claim her as your pet
Kick her as hard as you can
To prove you are a man
Get a small frightened animal
An act as every abuser criminal
Do not dwell on your black history
Lest you recognise the cat's misery
In seeing you as a speciesist molester
Think about Colston traders as investors
Trading slaves' blood for gold always festers
Using prejudice to sell their English history
The Zoumas sold their racist speciesism
Of *The Zong* and *Somerset* and their ancestors

An epitaph Zouma could share on Zoom
Chasing a scared cat around the room
At 15 stone and six feet four tried to score
Swearing *'I'll kill it'* is my life in the raw
Zouma reckons we have to understand
'I swear I'll kill it' was what he planned
Just because he is a footballer and a man
Doing what he wants because he thinks he can

Calling his cat 'it' proves it is a 'thing'
Exactly the same as a slave was in law
With a Jim Crow and Uncle Tom ring
Raw prejudice never ends in a draw

The Animals Film **Framed**

Let the skinny-ribbed dog keep barking
At the last abandoned caravan
The tight rope walker stole the elephant
Who cried non-stop on seeing the man
Ah but do I care
The ringmaster hit disaster ended up in plaster
Tripping over the prancing horse troop
Pierrot traded all the tears of a lifetime
For all the lions he had long since duped
Selling the monkeys as the circus moved on
As the last act of their unravelling betrayal
Unleashed a nightmare feel too strong to conceal
As *The Animals Film* started to freeze over
On the broken-down spinning reel-to-reel
The tragedy is over let the comedy begin

Bring on the dancing bears
Serve up my head on a plate
The Saturnalia is over
I have really lost a hold on fate
Ah but do I care
The Fat Lady's mirror shows the effigy
Of a stuffed hunted weasel and a wren
And the face has a trace of a sly smile
With a mean wish to meet crooked men
Estragon has been waiting in vain so long
He has faded into a neo-confessional den
The rebel-poet's wound will never heal
As *The Animals Film* is frozen forever
On the broken-down spinning reel-to-reel
The comedy is over let the tragedy begin

Index

A Creed of Claudette Colvin	166
A Deadhead Prize for Losers	55
A dog smiles with handcuffed teeth	81
A Dry Dog in a Wet Market	67
A Fish Out Of Water	127
A Gift Horse	64
Agnes Waterhouse was feared by neighbours	164
A Green River Killer Revisited	130
Albert learned while young	3
Albert Went Hunting	3
A Living Prize	29
All say 'sorry' as if a politician's plea	135
Although Jasmine and Jake	23
Although we know your aim	6
Animals Circling Space	81
A Number minus a Name	148
Anyone with a hoof	101
A Panther with a Panther	92
A Pigment of their Imagination	43
A Pope and a Pet	156
A Procrustean Apology	135
A Queen's Gambit	27
Arms Are Meant To Hold You	78

A Spotless Life	50
As with a terminal cancer	83
A Woman and a Hat and a Black Cat	119
Baby Fae and the Baboon	40
Black is the Colour	164
Burn the blue moon so it cries in the sky	121
Closing Bristol Zoo	99
Cock Crows into a Cocked Hat	60
Colston's Chains of Change	181
Colston paraded lies for 125 years	181
Cuckoo in the Mirror	85
DNA of a Politician	152
Dog Eat Dog	11
Duped By Descartes	44
Fired by her baptism	166
'Fishing is my way of breathing' said Ted Hughes	127
Flames licked her feet	119
Grandma what is a Gorilla	128
Heart to Heart	96
How Can a Man be another Man's Dog	172
How the people cheered when they heard	99
I had no choice in my form when being born	31
I hate water said the carp to the old trout	14
I never realised that just two eyes	126
In Good Company	122
In the blackness of night	137
In 2021 a cop in Italy	63
In 2022 in downtown Brunswick city	92
In 2022 a herd of bison	68

Is the Polar Jury still Out	86
I Swear I'll Kill It	183
It's a beautiful day	155
James Somerset escaped from his owner	172
Jews Don't Count	159
Jumping Judge	76
Jungle Judge Justice	103
Just Like Joe Exotic	72
Law of your Jungle	101
Let the skinny-ribbed dog keep barking	186
Life Can Get Lonely	31
Links to the Lynx	52
Loose Use of Language	89
Marathon mice raced against dementia	44
Mary Smith gazed out the window	50
Meet Me beneath the Magic of our Moon	126
M57	63
No Longer Born To Run	100
On 9 March 2022	43
Paulo the Pussyfooter	137
Prosopagnosia	98
Pshaw he said to the Irish	124
PTSD	8
Rees-Mogg asked Reg Presley	152
Robots Never Bleed	153
Salt of the Earth	57
Scapegoats towards Slaughter	150
Scavenging on the street for something to eat	67
Schrodinger's Cat	14

See the bright blood in the snow	64
Shafted By Fashion	80
She fell down the Stairs	23
She is too old to be of much use now	100
Standing in your furs 'n' your feathers 'n' minks	80
Stripe was starving to death	34
Stripping Stripe	34
Syphilis in Tuskegee	162
Target animals denied any escape	55
The advance of a rudderless ship	130
The animals figured enough was enough	21
The Animals Film Framed	186
The Arch was a man and a half	57
The baboon did not have a name	40
The Blackboard Jungle	133
The Bonds of Birth	37
The boy threw the hoop	29
The Chinese Academy of Sciences	38
The Chinese seek science without sleaze	148
The Clotilda sailed in 1859	141
The cock crowed since he was born	60
The crack of the whip	18
The diner considered he was a culinary expert	78
The First Thing we do is let's Kill all the Lawyers	21
The Good Death	32
The inability to recognise faces is a splendid gift	98
Their conspiracy cabal thrived	162
The Irish have good reason to hate the English	124
The lesson of their lives	37

The metal detector vivisectionist	153
The Octopus Met Sisyphus	48
The Pope sermonizing for our redemption	156
The prosecution jumped up to claim	76
The Question	83
There was a time not so long ago	128
The Russian looked at his opponent	27
The sleek beauty of the Eurasian lynx	52
The snow white real teddy bear	86
The soldier risked his life and limbs	8
The spilled sewage flowed free	88
The Spin We Are In	6
The Story of the Last Slave Barracoon	141
The teacher told the class	133
The Tiger King has a sordid ring	72
The whale is already fetid	176
They come along as burglars	85
They have lived a good life	32
They line up ready	150
Though few clung to the sharp deal	48
Time-bomb Heart	155
Too Much Monkey Business	38
Toxic Soup in the Tide	88
Unlike the President of South Korea	11
Vistal Garg wired his cute barb	122
We are supposed to marvel at a miracle	96
We Can See the Sea	176
What Am I Bid	146
When the wise judge said	89

Who Breaks a Butterfly upon a Wheel	16
Who breaks a butterfly upon a wheel	16
Why do You Love to Hate Me	10
Why do you want to make my start in life an end	10
Wild Things We Think We Love You	68
With or without an axe many claim	159
Without Elvis it was still Jailhouse Rock	146
Written in Water	121
You see my Bro and me	183
Zouma and Bro get their Kicks	18

About the Author

Noël Sweeney is a practising barrister who specializes in criminal law and human rights and animal law. He has lectured and written on all those subjects including in particular the legal role and status of animals.

Sweeney has presented his poems and songs on animal rights in bars and under the stars. While he is not prone to follow any particular person or creed, Sweeney does favour those who pursue the cause of justice for those unable to do so in their own right because they are branded by birth as victims of our prejudice.

Sweeney misses Cyril the squirrel who used to regularly visit and entertain the people with practised acrobatics. Although there are about a quarter of a million red squirrels and two-and-half million grey ones, to each one their life matters. A squirrel that is killed in jest, like the rest of us, dies in earnest.

www.ingramcontent.com/pod-product-compliance
Lightning Source LLC
Chambersburg PA
CBHW020107240426
43661CB00002B/56